# POPULAR
# MUSIC

# The Popular Music Series

*Popular Music, 1920–1979* is a revised cumulation of and supersedes Volumes 1 through 8 of the *Popular Music* series, of which Volumes 6 through 8 are still available:

*Popular Music, 1900–1919* is a companion volume to the revised cumulation.

This series continues with:

# Other Books by Bruce Pollock

*The Face of Rock and Roll: Images of a Generation*

*Hipper Than Our Kids?: A Rock and Roll Journal of the Baby Boom Generation*

*In Their Own Words: Popular Songwriting, 1955–1974*

*When Rock Was Young: The Heyday of Top 40*

*When the Music Mattered: Rock in the 1960s*

ISSN 0886-442X

VOLUME 18

1993

# POPULAR MUSIC

An Annotated Guide to American Popular Songs,
including Introductory Essay, Lyricists and Composers Index,
Important Performance Index, Awards Index,
and List of Publishers

BRUCE POLLOCK
Editor

Gale Research Inc. • DETROIT • WASHINGTON, D.C. • LONDON

Bruce Pollock, *Editor*

**Gale Research Inc. Staff**

Allison K. McNeill, *Developmental Editor*
Lawrence W. Baker, *Senior Developmental Editor, Popular Music Series*

Mary Beth Trimper, *Production Director*
Deborah L. Milliken, *Production Assistant*

Cynthia Baldwin, *Art Director*
Barbara J. Yarrow, *Graphic Design Supervisor*

Dennis LaBeau, *Editorial Data Systems Director*
Theresa Rocklin, *Program Design*
Benita L. Spight, *Manager, Data Entry Services*
Gwendolyn S. Tucker, *Data Entry Supervisor*
Nancy K. Sheridan, *Data Entry Associate*

This book is printed on acid-free paper that meets the minimum requirements of American National Standard for Information Sciences—Permanence Paper for Printed Library Materials, ANSI Z39.48-1984.

Library of Congress Catalog Card Number 85-653754
ISBN 0-8103-8498-1
ISSN 0886-442X

Published simultaneously in the United Kingdom
by Gale Research International Limited
(An affiliated company of Gale Research Inc.)

I⟨T⟩P™

The trademark **ITP** is used under license.

10 9 8 7 6 5 4 3 2 1

# Contents

# About the Book and How to Use It

This volume is the eighteenth of a series whose aim is to set down in permanent and practical form a selective, annotated list of the significant popular songs of our times. Other indexes of popular music have either dealt with special areas, such as jazz or theater and film music, or been concerned chiefly with songs that achieved a degree of popularity as measured by the music-business trade indicators, which vary widely in reliability.

## Annual Publication Schedule

The first nine volumes in the *Popular Music* series covered sixty-five years of song history in increments of five or ten years. Volume 10 initiated a new annual publication schedule, making background information available as soon as possible after a song achieves prominence. Yearly publication also allows deeper coverage—over five hundred songs—with additional details about writers' inspiration, uses of songs, album appearances, and more.

## Indexes Provide Additional Access

Three indexes make the valuable information in the song listings even more accessible to users. The Lyricists & Composers Index shows all the songs represented in *Popular Music, 1993,* that are credited to a given individual. The Important Performances Index (introduced in the revised cumulation *Popular Music, 1920–1979*) tells at a glance what albums, musicals, films, television shows, or other media-featured songs are represented in the volume. The "Performer" category—first added to the index as "Vocalist" in the 1986 volume—allows the user to see with what songs an artist has been associated this year. The index is arranged by broad media category, then alphabetically by the show or album title, with the songs listed under each title. Finally, the Awards Index (also introduced in the cumulation) provides a list of the songs nominated for awards by the

American Academy of Motion Picture Arts and Sciences (Academy Award) and the American Academy of Recording Arts and Sciences (Grammy Award). Winning songs are indicated by asterisks.

## List of Publishers

The List of Publishers is an alphabetically arranged directory providing addresses—when available—for the publishers of the songs represented in this eighteenth volume of *Popular Music*. Also noted is the organization handling performance rights for the publisher—in the United States, the American Society of Composers, Authors, and Publishers (ASCAP) or Broadcast Music, Inc. (BMI), and in Canada, the Society of Composers, Authors, and Music Publishers of Canada (SOCAN).

## Tracking Down Information on Songs

Unfortunately, the basic records kept by the active participants in the music business are often casual, inaccurate, and transitory. There is no single source of comprehensive information about popular songs, and those sources that do exist do not publish complete material about even the musical works with which they are directly concerned. Three of the primary proprietors of basic information about our popular music are the major performing rights societies—ASCAP, BMI, and SOCAN. Although each of these organizations has considerable information about the songs of its own writer and publisher members and has also issued indexes of its own songs, their files and published indexes are designed primarily for clearance identification by the commercial users of music. Their publications of annual or periodic lists of their "hits" necessarily include only a small fraction of their songs, and the facts given about these are also limited. ASCAP, BMI, and SOCAN are, however, invaluable and indispensable sources of data about popular music. It is just that their data and special knowledge are not readily accessible to the researcher.

Another basic source of information about musical compositions and their creators and publishers is the Copyright Office of the Library of Congress. There a computerized file lists each published, unpublished, republished, and renewed copyright of songs registered with the Office since 1979. This is helpful for determining the precise date of the declaration of the original ownership of musical works, but contains no other information. To complicate matters further, some authors, composers, and publishers have been known to employ rather makeshift methods of protecting their works legally, and there are songs listed in *Popular Music* that may not be found in the Library of Congress files.

## Selection Criteria

In preparing this series, the editor was faced with a number of separate problems. The first and most important of these was that of selection. The stated aim of the project—to offer the user as comprehensive and accurate a listing of significant popular songs as possible—has been the guiding criterion. The purpose has never been to offer a judgment on the quality of any songs or to indulge a prejudice for or against any type of popular music. Rather, it is the purpose of *Popular Music* to document those musical works that (1) achieved a substantial degree of popular acceptance, (2) were exposed to the public in especially notable circumstances, or (3) were accepted and given important performances by influential musical and dramatic artists.

Another problem was whether or not to classify the songs as to type. Most works of music are subject to any number of interpretations and, although it is possible to describe a particular performance, it is more difficult to give a musical composition a label applicable not only to its origin but to its subsequent musical history. In fact, the most significant versions of some songs are often quite at variance with their origins. Citations for such songs in *Popular Music* indicate the important facts about not only their origins but also their subsequent lives, rather than assigning an arbitrary and possibly misleading label.

## Research Sources

The principal sources of information for the titles, authors, composers, publishers, and dates of copyright of the songs in this volume were the Copyright Office of the Library of Congress, ASCAP, BMI, SOCAN, and individual writers and publishers. Data about best-selling recordings were obtained principally from three of the leading music business trade journals—*Billboard, Radio & Records,* and *Cash Box.* For the historical notes; information about foreign, folk, public domain, and classical origins; and identification of theatrical, film, and television introducers of songs, the editor relied upon collections of album notes, theater programs, sheet music, newspaper and magazine articles, and other material, both his own and that in the Lincoln Center Library for the Performing Arts in New York City.

## Contents of a Typical Entry

The primary listing for a song includes

- Title and alternate title(s)
- Country of origin (for non-U.S. songs)

- Author(s) and composer(s)
- Current publisher, copyright date
- Annotation on the song's origins or performance history

*Title:* The full title and alternate title or titles are given exactly as they appear on the Library of Congress copyright record or, in some cases, the sheet music. Since even a casual perusal of the book reveals considerable variation in spelling and punctuation, it should be noted that these are the colloquialisms of the music trade. The title of a given song as it appears in this series is, in almost all instances, the one under which it is legally registered.

*Foreign Origin:* If a song is of foreign origin, the primary listing indicates the country of origin after the title. Additional information may be noted, such as the original title, copyright date, writer, publisher in country of origin, or other facts about the adaptation.

*Authorship:* In all cases, the primary listing reports the author or authors and the composer or composers. The reader may find variations in the spelling of a songwriter's name. This results from the fact that some writers used different forms of their names at different times or in connection with different songs. These variants appear in the Lyricists & Composers Index as well. In addition to this kind of variation in the spelling of writers' names, the reader will also notice that in some cases, where the writer is also the performer, the name as a writer may differ from the form of the name used as a performer.

*Publisher:* The current publisher is listed. Since *Popular Music* is designed as a practical reference work rather than an academic study, and since copyrights more than occasionally change hands, the current publisher is given instead of the original holder of the copyright. If a publisher has, for some reason, copyrighted a song more than once, the years of the significant copyright subsequent to the year of the original copyright are also listed after the publisher's name.

*Annotation:* The primary listing mentions significant details about the song's history—the musical, film, or other production in which the song was introduced or featured and, where important, by whom it was introduced, in the case of theater and film songs; any other performers identified with the song; first or best-selling recordings and album inclusions, indicating the performer and the record company; awards; and other relevant data. The name of a performer may be listed differently in connection with different songs, especially over a period of years. The name listed is the form of the name given in connection with a particular performance or record. Dates are provided for important recordings and performances.

# Popular Music in 1993

Its dominance as a radio format and its relevance as a cultural determinant battered by all manner of number-crunchers and rock critics throughout much of 1993, the venerable Top 40's ultimate return to musical viability was the top story of the year, with echoes that will undoubtedly affect 1994 and beyond.

At its best a continuous national all-day and all-night hotline and switchboard of Americana, providing, in addition to the obvious musical mood of the populace, subtle style and fashion cues and clues for living, a secret coded language, the latest dance steps, and an ever-changing cast of characters and buzzwords, the Top 40, as a format and a musical framework capable of encompassing great variety, had suffered miserably through the early 1990's post-vinyl era of the rap, the sample, and the re-mix.

With virtually every segment of the population by now represented by a specific chart to reflect its particular heartbeats and mood swings, it was questionable as to whether the massive Top 40 could ever regain its stature as a musical melting pot. By mid-1993, it had become a repository only for a certain limited style of song, mainly rap, dance, and the occasional big movie ballad.

### Alternative Rock Invades Top 40

But in the last quarter of 1993, a whole new crop of red-blooded alternative rock and roll songs launched a siege on the charts reminiscent of the mid-'80s, when the Bangles and the Boss were furrowing their fevered folk/rock brows and Cyndi Lauper was out there having tons of fun. While this "whitelash" has been accomplished primarily at the expense of the more extreme forms of "gangsta" rap, it is also true that rock and roll has historically been moved through its changes almost as much by the so-called "alternative" sound of a jangly guitar (for example, Bob Dylan, the Byrds, and R.E.M.; James Burton, Scotty Moore, and the rockabilly sound of Elvis

Presley) as it has by the mixture of rhythms of the black underground (R&B, soul, disco, reggae, rap, hip hop, etc.).

By the end of 1993, with the message of "gangsta" rap effectively white-washed, the new jangly guitar phase of rock and roll was taking its place as the protest music of the overground culture, stamped for approval by Top 40. The Seattle sound got much of the early mainstream notice in this regard, with new material from the scene's two linchpins, Nirvana ("Heart Shaped Box") and Pearl Jam ("Daughter"), as well as their prime imitator, the Stone Temple Pilots ("Plush"). On the East Coast, the popular alterna-tive chalice was carried by the Spin Doctors ("Two Princes") and 10,000 Maniacs ("Candy Everybody Wants" and the swan song of their reigning doyenne, Natalie Merchant, "Because the Night," an unplugged cover of the Bruce Springsteen/Patti Smith alternative standard). But the real impe-tus for the new jangly sound probably emanated more from the Gin Blos-soms, whose pair of hits, "Hey Jealousy" and "Found Out About You," were the posthumous works of their late guitarist, Doug Hopkins.

These unlikely successes fueled a motorcade of alternative songs, ranging from the sloppily eloquent ("Loser" by Beck, "Creep" by Radiohead) to the elegantly retro ("No Rain" by Blind Melon, "Mr. Jones" by Counting Crows). Digable Planets ("Where I'm From") took up where last year's Alternative Black congregation, Arrested Development, left off. Jon Eas-dale's poignant "Work for Food" put Dramarama briefly into a long-deserved spotlight. The Lemonheads, last year's college band of the year, came back with a sophomore effort ("Into Your Arms"). The notion of a Classic Alternative style arrived, complete with forebears bearing new works. There was Paul Westerberg, the veritable elder statesman of the breed, late of the legendary Minneapolis band the Replacements ("Dice Behind Your Shades"). Also from the Twin Cities came the heroic, if ancient, Soul Asylum, with a breakthrough tune and video ("Runaway Train"). One-time establishment alternative tokens R.E.M. ("Man on the Moon"), Peter Gabriel ("Steam"), and U2 ("Stay [Faraway So Close]") became true members of that dubious society at last. Even early Byrds imi-tator Tom Petty, who was once considered alternative, found it easy to fit in ("Mary Jane's Last Dance").

### From 4 Non Blondes to 1 Whitney—A Big Year for Women

Many of these alternative voices belonged to women. The mid-80s ancestry of the Bangles's Beatlesque folk/rock could be heard in breakout tunes by Juliana Hatfield ("My Sister"), Belly ("Feed the Tree"), the Breeders ("Cannonball"), and the Cranberries ("Linger"). Linda Perry's anguished moan adorned the 4 Non Blondes epic "What's Up?" Out of the underground, the works of Victoria Williams were showcased by several alternative bands, among them Soul Asylum, who covered the tortured "Summer of Drugs." Jane Siberry's ethereal "Love Is Everything" cemented her reputation as a daring original artist. Notable debuts included Maria's Muldaur's daughter, Jenni ("Black Clouds") and the moody October Project ("Bury My Lovely"). Kate Bush, the crown princess of the alternative underground, released the lush and spacey "Eat the Music." No wonder one of the most notorious tracks of the '80s was rediscovered, refurbished, and repackaged this year, David Kaufman's odd gem, "88 Lines About 44 Women" by the Nails. Indeed, 88 lines wouldn't be enough to cover all of the incredible music produced by women this year.

Elsewhere on the national charts, women found favor in the less daring realm of the big ballad, the exemplar of all time being Whitney Houston's multi Grammy-winning remake of Dolly Parton's "I Will Always Love You" from the movie *The Bodyguard,* which concluded its run early in 1993, winding up as the longest-lasting number one tune in pop history. Whitney did a similar favor for Chaka Kahn, reviving "I'm Every Woman." "I Have Nothing" and "Run to You" rounded out her impressive showing. Not far off her record-breaking pace, Mariah Carey pitched "Dreamlover" and "Hero" to the top of the charts, and Janet Jackson displaced her unfortunate brother ("Free Willy," indeed) as the most commercial Jackson with the Grammy-winning "That's the Way Love Goes," the racy "If," and the Oscar-nominated "Again." Similar big-balladry propelled songwriter Diane Warren to another banner year with "I'll Never Get Over You Getting Over Me" for Expose, "By the Time This Night Is Over" for Kenny G. and Peabo Bryson, and "Love Can Move Mountains" for Celine Dion. Dion's remake of Jennifer Rush's "The Power of Love," along with her duet with Clive Griffin on "When I Fall in Love" from the movie *Sleepless in Seattle,* certainly made folks forget about the other Dion, DiMucci. Another movie gem was the Oscar-winning Peabo Bryson/Regina Belle duet on the Alan Menken/Tim Rice epic from *Aladdin,* "A Whole New World." A more spirited movie tune was turned in by the still spry Tina Turner, entitled "I Don't Wanna Fight," from her biopic, "What's Love Got to Do with It."

### Rock and Roll Seniors Still Goin' Strong

Other virtual senior citizens of the rock and pop arena held fast to their grip on the public's pulse, led by the forever youngish Rod Stewart, who updated Van Morrison's fine "Have I Told You Lately." Slightly younger, but no less mature, Sting was particularly pointed in "If I Ever Lose My Faith in You." Having long since offered us some pungent teenage memories in "The Summer of '69," Bryan Adams ought to be allowed admittance into this aging fraternity as well; "Please Forgive Me" was this year's calling card. Later in the year, in a casting coup, all three of these creaky gentlemen were teamed in the hit "All for Love" from *The Three Musketeers*. Michael Bolton's lock on the graying set continued undiminished in 1993, with the schmaltzy "Said I Loved You... But I Lied." Donald Fagen, part of one of the 1970's quirkiest supergroups, Steely Dan, returned to recording after nearly a decade's absence with "Teahouse on the Tracks." Over in the more vigorous hard rock genre, the ageless Aerosmith proved their lusty vigor three times over with "Cryin'," "Livin' on the Edge" and the utterly appropriate "Amazing." But the biggest kudos of all, as well as the biggest dressing room, belonged to the outsized Meat Loaf, who took up in mid-breath virtually where he left off in 1977, in the Jim Steinman pop operetta "I'd Do Anything for Love (But I Won't Do That)."

### Oldsters Search for Roots

Which didn't mean that every effort by an over-aged semi-famous come-back kid found instant access to the marketplace. Jackson Browne cried out "I'm Alive"; nobody cared. Jimmy Webb claimed he was "Too Young to Die," but only David Crosby, who covered the track, believed him. Blues-singer Tracy Nelson returned to her Delta roots with "Livin the Blues." Neil Diamond, in a paean to his Brill Building roots, charged up the old chestnut "You've Lost That Lovin' Feelin'." John Sebastian offered up his own tribute to his Greenwich Village roots in "Night Owl Cafe." Laura Nyro conjured up her primal female roots in "The Descent of Luna Rose." Funkadelic's one-time headmaster, George Clinton, tried to capitalize on the roots of our new rock and roll president (no relation) in "Paint the White House Black." By and large, people yawned. Just thirty years after the British Invasion changed the shape of pop music forever (especially in England), Paul McCartney was back again on wax, offering "Hope of Deliverance." The reunited Squeeze of Difford and Tilbrook were looking for "Everything in the World." Stone-alone Mick Jagger was a bit less stringent in his demands in "Don't Tear Me Up." His partner in crime, Keith Richards, also released the solo "Eileen," prompting hopes of a 1994 Stones tour (perhaps with the reunited Beatles as an opening act?). That prototypical angry "English Boy," Pete Townshend, joined the solo ranks this year as well, but it was with the revival of his all-purpose rock-(opera, album, movie, ballet, book, T-shirt, coffee mug) *Tommy*, the Broadway musical, that he would seek to solidify his reputation as England's premier rock songwriter ("I Believe My Own Eyes").

This accolade, however, would have to be wrested from the hands of the prolific Elvis Costello, who collaborated in 1993 with Michael Thomas Brodsky and the other members of classical music's The Brodsky Quartet on *The Juliet Letters* ("I Almost Had a Weakness"), teamed with Paul McCartney ("The Lovers That Never Were"), saw one of his classics revived by Carter USM ("Peace in Our Time"), and wrote an entire album for a girl-singer, Wendy James ("This Is a Test").

Just about the only legend having a better year would be Bob Dylan, who moved from his thirtieth anniversary celebration last year to the release of the record to commemorate it, resulting in his Grammy-nominated performance of "My Back Pages," along with protest era pals Roger McGuinn, Tom Petty, George Harrison, Neil Young, and Eric Clapton. The most classic of any Classic Alternative icon, Dylan's newly refurbished rep has undoubtedly benefitted from—if not directly inspired—the fresh alternative winds coursing through the popular ozone. This year, Dylan bequeathed his legacy freely, without regard to race, creed, or recompense. Well, maybe recompense. He didn't exactly give away the use of "The Times They Are a Changin'" to an accounting firm for their commercial for pennies a day. Elsewhere, however, Aaron Neville crooned "Don't Fall Apart on Me Tonight" on the black charts, P. J. Harvey offered "Highway 61 Revisited" on the college charts, Judy Collins dipped back to 1963 for "Bob Dylan's Dream" and many others on her album of Bob covers, and country squire Willie Nelson teamed up with Bob himself on a couple of tunes, including "Heartland."

The jangly sound of country music was all in the cash registers this year, if not particularly high on the singles chart. If Garth Brooks ("Learning to Live Again"), Alan Jackson ("Chattahoochee"), and Dolly Parton ("Romeo") failed to capitalize on Billy Ray Cyrus's 1992 achy-break-through with the youth of America, they were happy to appeal to an older constituency that could think of country in the same breath as folk and bluegrass, folk/rock, and middle of the dirt road pop. Mary-Chapin Carpenter is the clear leader of this ring; her version of Lucinda Williams's "Passionate Kisses" arose from last year's album cuts into hit status and enduring fame as a Grammy winner for Best Country Song.

### Country + Folk + Rock + Pop = Adult Album Alternative

In fact, the type of music I call Middle of the Dirt Road gained a radio format all its own this year, called Adult Album Alternative, where country and folk join hands with rock and pop to form a kind of pop alternative mixture that any musically-aware adult could find challenging. At the country end of the spectrum, there was the Hank Williams Jr. lament, "Everything Comes Down to Money and Love," Joe Henry's unique "Fireman's Wedding," the annual Rosanne Cash confessional, "You Won't Let Me In," Suzy Bogguss' cover of John Hiatt's "Drive South," or Hiatt's own

xv

"Perfectly Good Guitar." At the pop/rock end of the dial, John Mellencamp completed his full transition to the middle of the dirt road ("Human Wheels"), Neil Young occasionally calmed down enough to visit ("Harvest Moon"), and even Billy Joel paid for his admission with his songwriting stripes ("River of Dreams," "No Man's Land"). Folkies, both lapsed and relapsed, found the middle of the dirt road an appropriate resting place from the rigors of the relentless cutting edge. Grammy-winner Nanci Griffith dusted off some treasures of this repertoire, including John Prine's "Speed of the Sound of Loneliness" and Frank Christian's "Three Flights Up." Iris DeMent veered near bluegrass purity ("Infamous Angel," "Our Town"). The incomparable acoustic sound of the Bobs was at an incomparable peak ("Angels of Mercy"). The Story graduated from coffeehouse obscurity to big-label authenticity ("So Much Mine"). Patti Larkin added to her reputation as a troubadour ("Pundits and Poets"), while Darden Smith actually had a cup of coffee on the pop charts ("Lovin' Arms"). The man who once found a dead skunk in the middle of the dirt road, Loudon Wainwright III, gave us more insight into his ongoing neurotic autobiography ("Sometimes I Forget").

### Bad Boy Rappers Look for Escape

No less word-obsessed were this year's declasse rappers, who, in their abundance and arrogance, failed to heed the warning of their godfather, Ice-Cube, to "Check Yo Self." As tough and streetwise as they wanted to be, they proceeded to find enough rope with which to hang themselves in the public eye. Tupac Shakur, for instance, will not be remembered for 1993's inspirational "Keep Ya Head Up," but instead for the assault conviction against him that began in 1994. Dr. Dre was nothing but authentic in hits like "Nuthin' But a `G' Thang," "Dre Day," and "Let Me Ride," but his protege, Snoop Doggy Dogg (known to his mother as Calvin Broadus) had to significantly neuter his own solo hit, "What's My Name," to get it on the radio. That would be the least of his problems; as the year ended he was also a candidate for Court TV as an accomplice in a shooting. And yet, the rage that produced "Slam" by Onyx or "Six Feet Deep" by the Geto Boys was not at all diluted by an unprofane but heartfelt tribute to some fallen friends from the old neighborhood in DRS's "Gangsta Lean."

In using their art as a defense against the real life blues of survival in the ghetto, many black artists chose to escape. Some got high ("Insane in the Brain" by Cypress Hill). Some watched too much TV ("Dazzey Duks" by Duice, based on the Daisy Duke character from the old TV show "The Dukes of Hazzard"). Some played hoops ("I Know I Got Skillz" by the Orlando Magic's Shaquille O'Neal). Others sat in the audience ("Whoomp! [There It Is]" by Tag Team and "Whoot, There It Is" by 95 South, both songs becoming by year's end something like the musical equivalent of The Wave). As usual, the best form of escapism was sex—from Positive K's robust dialogue, "I Got a Man," to Salt-N-Pepa's new innuendo, "Shoop." More typically, the sex was as raw as the following titles would suggest: "Sex Me (Parts I and II)" by R. Kelly, "Come Baby Come" by K7, and "Come Inside" by Intro. (Sexual escapism was by no means restricted to rappers, however, as evidenced by "Come Undone" by Duran Duran, and the ever-sexy "Come to Butt-Head" by MTV's resident cartoonheads, Beavis and Butt-Head).

Better than sex, pure talent is an even sweeter revenge. In this context, Kenny Edmunds, also known as Babyface, had the best of years, as a singer and a songwriter, whether writing by himself ("Breathe Again" for Toni Braxton), collaborating with Duane Simmons ("Can We Talk" for Tevin Campbell, "Another Sad Love Song" for Toni Braxton), or writing and singing by himself, for himself ("Never Keeping Secrets" and "Something in Your Eyes").

### International Flavor from Reggae and Broadway

Almost as sweet was this year's long-awaited reggae breakthrough, featuring a multiracial multitude of international performers, among them Snow from Canada ("Informer"), Ace of Base from Sweden ("All That She Wants"), the legendary Jimmy Cliff from Jamaica ("I Can See Clearly Now"), the ubiquitous UB40 from England ("Can't Help Falling in Love"), and Ian Lewis's Inner Circle from Miami ("Sweat," "Bad Boys").

What little there is to be said about the Broadway season had an international accent as well, with three of the four enduring musicals emanating from foreign soil. England gave us *Blood Brothers* ("Tell Me It's Not True") and the aforementioned *Tommy.* Holland's *Cyrano* ("Even Then") survived a somewhat bumpy crossing. Even Kander & Ebb's *Kiss of the Spider Woman* ("The Day After That") took place in South America.

### Movie Moments—Better Than Popcorn

In the movies, 1993 provided considerably more gratifying moments. In *Philadelphia,* for instance, there was a Bruce Springsteen song ("Streets of Philadelphia") winning both a Golden Globe and an Oscar, and a Neil Young song being nominated for an Oscar ("Philadelphia"). Annie Ross covered the Doc Pomus/Dr. John tune "Prisoner of Life" over the closing credits of Robert Altman's movie *Short Cuts.* Then there was an unlikely pair of Scottish brothers—the Reids, Charlie and Craig, and the Youngs, Angus and Malcolm—who co-wrote tunes for movies as disparate as *Benny and Joon* ("I'm Gonna Be [500 Miles]" by the Proclaimers) and *The Last*

*Action Hero* ("Big Gun" by AC/DC). None of these moments, of course, achieved anything like the perfect symmetry of Boy George's wonderful comeback as he crooned a 1964 English hit as the title tune from the oddly compelling *The Crying Game.*

*Bruce Pollock*
*Editor*

# A

**Again**
Words and music by Janet Jackson, James Harris, III, and Terry Lewis.
Black Ice Music, 1993/Flyte Tyme Tunes, 1993.
Best-selling record by Janet Jackson from the film *Poetic Justice* and
the album *janet* (Virgin, 93). Tune went to number one. Nominated
for an Academy Award, Best Song of the Year, 1993.

**Ain't Going Down (Til the Sun Comes Up)**
Words and music by Kent Blazy, Kim Williams, and Garth Brooks.
Sophie's Choice Music, 1993/Sony Cross Keys Publishing Co. Inc.,
1993/Major Bob Music, 1993/No Fences Music, 1993.
Best-selling record by Garth Brooks from *Pieces* (Liberty, 93).

**Ain't That Lonely Yet**
Words and music by Kostas and Jerry House.
Songs of Polygram, 1993/Sony Tree, 1993/Madwoman, 1993/Seven
Angels, 1993.
Best-selling record by Dwight Yoakam from *This Time* (Reprise, 93).
Nominated for a Grammy Award, Country Song of the Year, 1993.

**Alibis**
Words and music by Randy Boudreaux.
Sony Tree, 1993/Thanxamillion, 1993.
Best-selling record by Tracy Lawrence from *Alibis* (Atlantis, 93).

**All About Soul**
Words and music by Billy Joel.
Impulsive Music, 1993/EMI-April Music, 1993.
Best-selling record by Billy Joel from *River of Dreams* (Columbia, 93).

**All for Love** (Canadian-English)
Words and music by Bryan Adams, Robert John Lange, and Michael
Kamen.
Almo Music Corp., 1993/Zomba Music, 1993/Sony Songs, 1993/
Wonderland Music, 1993/Worksongs, 1993/K-Man, 1993.

Best-selling record by Bryan Adams, Rod Stewart, and Sting in the film and soundtrack album *The Three Musketeers* (Hollywood/A & M, 93).

**All I Want**
Words and music by Jason Bieler.
Love Tribe Music, 1992/MCA Music, 1993.
Introduced by Saigon Kick on *The Lizard* (Third Stone/Atlantic, 92).

**All That She Wants** (Swedish)
English words and music by Joker and Buddha.
Megasongs, 1992/BMG Music, 1992.
Best-selling record by Ace of Base from *The Sign* (Arista, 93). Song was a hit in several countries.

**All These Years**
Words and music by Mac McAnally.
Beginner Music, 1992.
Best-selling record by Sawyer Brown from *Cafe on the Corner* (Curb, 92).

**Almost Goodbye**
Words and music by Billy Livsey and Don Schlitz.
Irving Music Inc., 1993/Don Schlitz Music, 1993/New Hayes Music, 1993.
Best-selling record by Mark Chesnutt from *Almost Goodbye* (MCA, 93).

**Almost Unreal** (Swedish)
English words and music by Per Gessle.
EMI-Blackwood Music Inc., 1992/Jimmie Fun, 1993.
Introduced by Roxette in the film and soundtrack LP *Super Mario Brothers* (Capitol, 93).

**Alright**
Words and music by Jermaine Dupri.
EMI-April Music, 1993/So So Def Music, 1993.
Best-selling record by Kris Kross from *Da Bomb* (Ruffhouse/Columbia, 93).

**Amazing**
Words and music by Steven Tyler and Richard Supa.
Swag Song Music, 1993/Colgems-EMI Music, 1993/Super Supa Songs, 1993.
Best-selling record by Aerosmith from *Get a Grip* (Geffen, 93).

**American Honky Tonk Bar Association**
Words and music by Brian Kennedy and Jim Rushing.

EMI-April Music, 1993/The Old Professor's, 1993.
Best-selling record by Garth Brooks from *Pieces* (Liberty, 93).

### Angel
Words and music by Jon Secada and Miguel Morejon.
Estefan Music, 1992/Foreign Imported, 1993.
Best-selling record by Jon Secada from *Jon Secada* (SBK, 92).

### The Angel in the House
Words and music by Jonatha Brooke and Duke Levine.
Dog Dream, 1993.
Introduced by The Story in *The Angel in the House* (Electra, 93).

### Angels of Mercy
Words and music by Richard Greene.
Best of Breed Music, 1989.
Introduced by The Bobs on *Shut up and Sing* (Rounder, 93).

### Anniversary
Words and music by Raphael Wiggins and Carl Wheeler.
Polygram International, 1993/Tony! Toni! Tone!, 1993/Rev, 1993.
Best-selling record by Tony! Toni! Tone! on *Sons of Soul* (Wing/
    Mercury, 93). Nominated for a Grammy Award, Best R&B Song of
    the Year, 1993.

### Anodyne
Words and music by Jay Farrar and Jeff Tweedy.
VER Music, 1993/Freedom Songs, 1993/Warner-Tamerlane Music,
    1993.
Introduced by Uncle Tupelo on *Anodyne* (Sire, 93).

### Another Sad Love Song
Words and music by Babyface (pseudonym for Kenny Edmunds) and
    Daryl Simmons.
Ecaf, 1993/Sony Songs, 1993/Boobie Loo, 1993/Warner-Tamerlane
    Music, 1993.
Best-selling record by Toni Braxton from *Toni Braxton* (LaFace/Arista,
    93).

### Are You Gonna Go My Way
Words and music by Lenny Kravitz and Craig Ross.
Miss Bessie Music, 1993/Wigged Music, 1993.
Best-selling record by Lenny Kravitz from *Are You Gonna Go My Way*
    (Virgin, 93). Nominated for a Grammy Award, Best Rock Song of the
    Year, 1993.

### As If We Never Said Goodbye
Words and music by Andrew Lloyd Webber, Don Black, Christopher
    Hampton, and Amy Powers.

3

Music by Candlelight, 1993/PSO Ltd., 1993.
Performed by Barbra Streisand on *The Broadway Album* (Columbia, 93).

### As Long As I Can Dream
Words and music by Diane Warren and Roy Orbison.
Realsongs, 1989/Orbisongs, 1993.
Introduced by Expose on *Expose* (Arista, 93).

### Award Tour
Words and music by J. Davis, A. Muhammed, and M. Taylor.
Zomba Music, 1993/Jazz Merchant Music, 1993.
Introduced by A Tribe Called Quest on *Midnight Marauders* (Jive/BMG, 93).

# B

**Baby I'm Yours**
Words and music by Carl Martin and Marc Gay.
Music of the World, 1992/Gasoline Alley Music, 1992/Cameo
  Appearance by Ramses, 1992/MCA Music, 1992/Ethyl, 1992.
Best-selling record by Shai from *If I Ever Fall in Love* (Gasoline Alley/
  MCA, 92).

**Back to the Hotel**
Words and music by Johnny Zunino, James Trujillo, and Timothy Lyon.
Promuse, 1992/Deep Groove, 1992/Vogue Music, 1992.
Best-selling record by N2Deep from *Back to the Hotel* (Profile, 92).

**Bad Boys**
Words and music by Inner Circle.
Rock Pop Music, 1992.
Best-selling record by Inner Circle from the LP *Inner Circle* (Big Beat/
  Atlantic, 93). From the TV show *Cops*.

**Bad Girl**
Words and music by Madonna Ciccone and Shep Pettibone.
WB Music, 1992/Webo Girl, 1992/Shepsongs, 1992/MCA Music, 1992.
Best-selling record by Madonna from *Erotica* (Maverick/Sire, 92).

**A Bad Goodbye**
Words and music by Clint Black.
Blackened, 1993.
Best-selling record by Clint Black with Wynonna from *No Time to Kill*
  (MCA, 93).

**Be Somewhere**
Words by Marsha Norman, music by Jule Styne.
MCA Music, 1993.
Introduced by Hugh Panaro in the musical *The Red Shoes*.

**Beautiful Homes**
Words and music by Chris Isaak.

C. Isaak, 1993.
Introduced by Chris Isaak on *San Francisco Days* (Reprise, 93).

**Because the Night**
Words and music by Bruce Springsteen and Patti Smith.
Bruce Springsteen Publishing, 1978.
Revived by 10,000 Maniacs on *Unplugged* (Elektra, 93).

**Bed of Roses**
Words and music by Jon Bon Jovi.
Polygram International, 1992/Bon Jovi Publishing, 1993.
Best-selling record by Bon Jovi from *Keep the Faith* (Jambco/Mercury
    92).

**Being Simple**
Words and music by Jeff Heiskell, words and music by The Judybats.
Reach Around Music, 1993.
Introduced by The Judybats on *Pain Makes You Beautiful* (Sine/WB 93).

**Better Than You**
Words and music by Lisa Keith and Keith Thomas.
New Perspective Publishing, Inc., 1993/Sony Music, 1993/Yellow
    Elephant Music, 1993.
Best-selling record by Lisa Keith from *Walkin' in the Sun* (Perspective/
    A&M, 93).

**Big Gun** (Australian)
Words and music by Angus Young and Malcolm Young.
J. Albert & Sons Music, 1993.
Introduced by AC/DC on the film and soundtrack album *The Last
    Action Hero* (Columbia, 93).

**Black**
Words and music by Pearl Jam.
Innocent Bystander Music, 1991/Write Treatage Music, 1991.
Best-selling record by Pearl Jam from *Ten* (Epic, 91).

**Black Clouds**
Words and music by Jenni Muldaur and Brad Bailey.
Warner-Tamerlane Music, 1993/Little Reata, 1993/Sound Mind & Body,
    1993/King Kino, 1993.
Introduced by Jenni Muldaur on *Jenni Muldaur* (Warner Bros., 93)

**Black Gold**
Words and music by Dave Pirner.
WB Music, 1992/LFR Music, 1992.
Introduced by Soul Asylum on *Grave Dancers Union* (Columbia, 92).

**Blame It on Your Heart**
Words and music by Harlan Howard and Kostas.
Harlan Howard Songs, 1993/Sony Tree, 1993/Songs of Polygram, 1993/
 Seven Angels, 1993.
Best-selling record by Patty Loveless from *Only What I Feel* (Epic, 93).

**Bob Dylan's Dream**
Words and music by Bob Dylan.
Special Rider Music, 1963.
Revived by Judy Collins on *Judy Sings Dylan...Just Like a Woman*
 (Geffen, 93).

**Boom! Shake the Room**
Words and music by Will Smith, Mervin Pierce, Norman Napier, Walter
 Morrison, Marshall Jones, Gregory Webster, Leroy Bonner, Robert
 Middlebrooks, and Andrew McLain.
Zomba Music, 1993/Jazzy Jeff & Fresh Prince, 1993/House Jam, 1993/
 Forty Floors Up, 1993/Deshane, 1993/Bridgeport Music Inc., 1993.
Best-selling record by Jazzy Jeff & Fresh Prince from *Code Red* (Jive,
 93).

**Boomerang**
Words and music by Jenni Muldaur, Scott Mathews, and Bob Miller.
Warner-Tamerlane Music, 1993/Little Reata, 1993/Sound Mind & Body,
 1993/Hang Onto Your Publishing, 1993/Bug Music, 1993/Miching
 Mallecko, 1993.
Introduced by Jenni Muldaur on *Jenni Muldaur* (Warner Bros., 93).

**Both Sides of the Story** (English)
Words and music by Phil Collins.
Phil Collins, 1993/Hit & Run Music, 1993.
Best-selling record by Phil Collins from *Both Sides of the Story*
 (Atlantic, 93).

**Bottle It up and Go,** see **Step It up and Go.**

**Break It down Again** (English)
Words and music by Roland Orzabel and Alan Griffiths.
EMI-Virgin, 1993/Chrysalis Music Group, 1993.
Best-selling record by Tears for Fears from *Elemental* (Mercury, 93).

**Breathe Again**
Words and music by Babyface (pseudonym for Kenny Edmunds).
Ecaf, 1993/Sony Songs, 1993.
Best-selling record by Toni Braxton from *Toni Braxton* (Laface/Arista,
 93).

**Buffalo River Home**
Words and music by John Hiatt.

7

Lillybilly, 1993/Bug Music, 1993.
Introduced by John Hiatt on *Perfectly Good Guitar* (A&M, 93).

**Bury My Lovely**
Words and music by Julie Flanders and Emil Adler.
Famous Music Corp., 1993/October Project, 1993.
Introduced by October Project on *October Project* (Epic, 93).

**By the Time This Night Is Over**
Words and music by Michael Bolton, Diane Warren, and Andy
  Goldmark.
Warner-Tamerlane Music, 1993/Realsongs, 1993/New Nonpariel, 1993.
Best-selling record by Kenny G. and Peabo Bryson from *Breathless*
  (Arista, 93).

# C

**Calling All Angels** (Canadian)
Words and music by Jane Siberry.
Wing It, 1991/Bug Music, 1991.
Revivived by Jane Siberry and k.d. lang on *When I Was a Boy* (Reprise, 93).

**Calling to You** (English)
Words and music by Robert Plant and Otis Blackwell.
Copyright Control, 1993.
Best-selling record by Robert Plant from *Fate of Nations* (Es Paranza/ Atlantic, 93).

**Can I Trust You with My Heart**
Words and music by Travis Tritt and Stuart Harris.
Sony Tree, 1992/Post Oak, 1992/Edisto Music, 1992.
Best-selling record by Travis Tritt from *T-R-O-U-B-L-E* (Warner Bros., 91).

**Can We Talk**
Words and music by Babyface (pseudonym for Kenny Edmunds) and Daryl Simmons.
Ecaf, 1993/Sony Songs, 1993/Boobie Loo, 1993/Warner-Tamerlane Music, 1993.
Best-selling record by Tevin Campbell from *I'm Ready* (Owert, 93).
Nominated for a Grammy Award, R&B Song of the Year, 1993.

**Can You Forgive Her** (English)
Words and music by Nick Tennant and Chris Lowe.
Virgin Music Ltd., 1993.
Introduced by Pet Shop Boys on *Very* (EMI/ERG, 93).

**Candle in the Wind** (English)
Words and music by Elton John and Bernie Taupin.
Intersong, USA Inc., 1973/Big Pig Music, 1973.

Revived by Kate Bush (Columbia). Song is on the flipside of 'Eat for Music' single.

**Candy Everybody Wants**
Words and music by Natalie Merchant and Dennis Drew.
Christian Burial Music, 1993.
Revived by 10,000 Maniacs on *Unplugged* (Elektra, 93).

**Cannonball**
Words and music by Kim Deal.
Period Music, 1993.
Best-selling record by The Breeders on *Last Splash* (4 A.D/Elektra, 93).

**Can't Break It to My Heart**
Words and music by Kirk Roth, Tracy Lawrence, Earl Clark, and Elbert West.
Loggy Bayou Music, 1993/Mike Dunn, 1993/JMV Music Inc., 1993.
Best-selling record by Tracy Lawrence from *Alibis* (Atlantic, 93).

**Can't Do a Thing (to Stop Me)**
Words and music by Chris Isaak and Brian Elliot.
Issac, 1993/Brian Elliot, 1993.
Introduced by Chris Isaak on *San Francisco Days* (Reprise, 93).

**Can't Get Enough of Your Love**
Words and music by Barry White.
Unichappell Music Inc., 1974.
Revived by Taylor Dayne on *Soul Dancing* (Arista, 93).

**Can't Help Falling in Love**
Words and music by George Weiss, Hugo Peretti, and Luigi Creatore.
Gladys Music, 1961/Williamson Music, 1961.
Revived by UB40 in the film and soundtrack album *Sliver* (Virgin, 93).

**Cat's in the Cradle**
Words and music by Harry Chapin and Sandy Chapin.
Story Songs Ltd., 1974.
Revived by Ugly Kid Joe from *America's Least Wanted* (Stardog/Mercury, 92).

**Chattahoochee**
Words and music by Alan Jackson and Jim McBride.
Mattie Ruth Musick, 1992/Seventh Son Music, 1992/Sony Cross Keys Publishing Co. Inc., 1992.
Best-selling record by Alan Jackson from *A Lot About Livin' (and a Little 'Bout Love)* (Arista, 92). Nominated for a Grammy Award, Best Country Song of the Year, 1993.

**Check Yo Self**
Words and music by Ice Cube and Larry Muggurud.
WB Music, 1992/Gangsta Boogie, 1992/MCA Music, 1992/Soul
   Assassins Music, 1992.
Best-selling record by Ice Cube featuring Das EFX from *The Predator*
   (Priority, 92). A relatively tame year from the father of 'Gangsta' rap.

**Choice of Colours**
Words and music by Curtis Mayfield.
Warner-Tamerlane Music, 1969.
Revived by Jerry Butler on *People Get Ready: A Tribute to Curtis
   Mayfield* (Shanachee, 93). Butler and Mayfield used to sing together
   in the Impressions.

**Closing Time** (Canadian)
Words and music by Leonard Cohen.
Leonard Cohen Stranger Music Inc., 1992.
Introduced by Leonard Cohen on *The Future* (Virgin, 92).

**C'mon Everybody**
Words and music by Eddie Cochran and Jerry Capeheart.
Unart Music Corp., 1958.
Revived by NRBQ on *The Best of NRBQ-Stay with Me* (Columbia/
   Legacy, 93).

**C'mon People** (English)
Words and music by Paul McCartney.
MPL Communications Inc., 1993.
Introduced by Paul McCartney on *Off the Ground* (Capitol, 92).

**Come Baby Come**
Words and music by K7, words and music by Joey Gardner.
Tee Girl Music, 1993/Blue Ink, 1993/Third and Lex, 1993.
Best-selling record by K7 from *Swing Batta Swing* (Tommy Boy, 93).

**Come Inside**
Words and music by Kenny Greene, Clint Wike, and Nevelle Hodge.
Velle Int'l, 1993/Frabensha, 1993/MCA Music, 1993/Ness, Nitty &
   Capone, 1993/WB Music, 1993/Wike, 1993.
Best-selling record by Intro from *Intro* (Atlantic, 93).

**Come to Butt-Head**
Words and music by Mike Judge and Nile Rodgers.
Judgemental Music, 1993/Tommy Jymi, Inc., 1993.
Introduced by Beavis and Butt-Head in *The Beavis and Butt-Head
   Experience* (Geffen, 93). One part Siskel and Ebert, one part Wayne's
   World, MTV's cartoon critics capitalize on their newfound fame.

**Come Undone** (English)
Words and music by Duran Duran.
Copyright Control, 1993.
Best-selling record by Duran Duran from *Duran Duran* (Capitol, 93).

**Comforter**
Words and music by Carl Martin, Marc Gay, and Dannell VanRensalier.
Music Corp. of America, 1992/Gasoline Alley Music, 1992.
Best-selling record by Shai from *If I Ever Fall in Love* (Gasoline Alley/
    MCA,92).

**Connected**
Words and music by Rob Birch, Nick Hallan, Harry Casey, and Rick
    Finch.
EMI-Virgin, 1993/Harrick Music Inc., 1993/Longitude Music, 1993.
Best-selling record by Stereo MC's from *Connected* (Gee Street/Island,
    93).

**Country at War**
Words and music by John Doe.
Warner-Tamerlane Music, 1993/Faith Hope and Charity, 1993.
Introduced by X on *Hey Zeus* (Big Life/Mercury, 93).

**Crazy Mary**
Words and music by Victoria Williams.
Mumblety Peg, 1993/Careers-BMG, 1993.
Revived by Pearl Jam on *Sweet Relief: A Benefit for Victoria Williams*
    (Chaos/Columbia, 93).

**Creep** (English)
Words and music by Radiohead.
Warner-Chappell Music, 1993/WB Music, 1993.
Best-selling record by Radiohead from *Pablo Honey* (Capitol, 93).

**Cruel Little Number** (Canadian)
Words and music by Jeff Healey, Joe Rockman, Tom Stephen, Carl
    Marsh, and Justis Walker.
See the Light, 1992/Hamstein Music, 1992/Eighth Nerve, 1992/Red
    Brazos, 1992.
Best-selling record by The Jeff Healey Band from *Feel This* (Arista,
    92).

**Cry for You**
Words and music by DeVante Swing.
EMI-April Music, 1993/Deswing Mob, 1993.
Best-selling record by Jodeci from *Diary of a Mad Band* (Uptown/
    MCA, 93).

**Cryin'**
Words and music by Steven Tyler, Joe Perry, and Taylor Rhodes.
Swag Song Music, 1993/MCA Music, 1993/Taylor Rhodes Music, 1993.
Best-selling record by Aerosmith from *Get a Grip* (Geffen, 93).
   Nominated for a Grammy Award, Rock Song of the Year, 1993.

**The Crying Game**
Words and music by Geoff Stephens.
Southern Music Publishing Co., Inc., 1965.
Revived by Boy George in the film and soundtrack album of *The Crying Game* (SBR, 93).

**Crying in the Rain**
Music by Carole King, words by Howie Greenfield.
Screen Gems-EMI Music Inc., 1961/Careers-BMG, 1961.
Revived by Art Garfunkel with James Taylor in *Up Til Now* (Columbia, 93).

**Cursed Female**
Words and music by Porno for Pyros.
EMI-Virgin, 1993/I'll Hit You Back, 1993.
Best-selling record BY Porno for Pyros from *Porno for Pyros* (Warner Bros., 93).

# D

**Daughter**
Words and music by Pearl Jam.
Innocent Bystander Music, 1993/Write Treatage Music, 1993/Scribing
  C-Ment Music, 1993/Pickled Fish Music, 1993/Jumping Cat Music,
  1993.
Introduced by Pearl Jam on *Vs* (Epic Associated, 93).

**The Day After That**
Music by John Kander, words by Fred Ebb.
Fiddleback, 1989/Kander & Ebb Inc., 1989.
Introduced by Anthony Crivello in *Kiss of the Spider Woman* (93).
  Released by Liza Minnelli (Sony, 93). Used as the anthem for the
  American Foundation for AIDS research.

**The Day I Fall in Love**
Words and music by Carole Bayer-Sager, music by James Ingram and
  Clint Magness.
All About Me Music, 1993/Music of the World, 1993/Yah-Mo, 1993/
  Warner-Tamerlane Music, 1993/WB Music, 1993/Magnified, 1993/
  MCA Music, 1993.
Introduced by Dolly Parton and James Ingram in the film and
  soundtrack to *Beethoven's 2nd* (Columbia, 93). Nominated for an
  Academy Award, Best Song of the Year, 1993.

**Dazzey Duks**
Words and music by L.A. Sno, D. Creole, and Troy Taylor.
Gigolo Chez Publishing, 1992/Alvert Music, 1992.
Best-selling record by Duice from *Dazzey Duks* (TMR, 93). Based on
  the character of Daisy Duke from the TV show 'The Dukes of
  Hazzard.'

**Dear One**
Music by John Kander, words by Fred Ebb.
Fiddleback, 1989/Kander & Ebb Inc., 1989.

Introduced by Chita Rivera in *Kiss of the Spider Woman* (93) and on the cast album (RCA, 93).

**Dedicated**
Words and music by Robert Kelly.
Willesden Music, Inc., 1992/R. Kelly Music, 1992.
Best-selling record by R. Kelly & Public Announcement from *Born into the '90s* (Jive, 92).

**Delicate** (English)
Words and music by Terence Trent D'arby.
Monosteri Music, 1993/EMI-Virgin, 1993.
Best-selling record by Terence Trent D'arby from *Symphony or Damn* (Columbia, 93).

**The Descent of Luna Rose**
Words and music by Laura Nyro.
Luna Mist Music, 1993.
Introduced by Laura Niro on *Walk the Dog & Lite the Lite (Run the Dog Darling Lite Delite)* (Columbia, 93).

**The Devil You Know** (English)
Words and music by Jesus Jones.
EMI-Blackwood Music Inc., 1993.
Best-selling record by Jesus Jones from *Perverse* (SBK/ERG, 93).

**Dice Behind Your Shades**
Words and music by Paul Westerberg.
Elegant Mule, 1993.
Introduced by Paul Westerberg on *14 Songs* (Sire/Reprise, 93).

**Ditty**
Words and music by J. Ferguson, D. Ferguson, Aaron Clark, Mitchell Johnson, and David Weldon.
Cisum Ludes, 1993/Saja Music Co., 1993/Troutman's, 1993.
Best-selling record by Paperboy from *Nine Yards* (Next Plateau, 93).

**Does He Love You**
Words and music by Sandy Knox and Billy Stritch.
PKM Music, 1982/Golden Reed Music, 1982/New Clarion, 1982.
Best-selling record by Reba McEntire with Linda Davis from *Greatest Hits, Volume Two* (MCA, 93). Nominated for a Grammy Award, Country Song of the Year, 1993.

**Dogs of Lust** (English)
Words and music by Matt Johnson.
Lazarus Ltd. (England), 1993/Sony Music, 1993.
Best-selling record by The The from *Dusk* (Epic, 93).

**Don't Fall Apart on Me Tonight**
Words and music by Bob Dylan.
Special Rider Music, 1983.
Revived by Aaron Neville on *The Grand Tour* (A&M, 93).

**Don't Look Now**
Words and music by David Williams, Andrew Williams, and Marvin
    Etzioni.
PSO Ltd., 1993/Sky Garden Music, 1993/Prophet Sharing Music, 1993/
    Famous Music Corp., 1993/Blue Saint Music, 1993.
Introduced by The Williams Brothers on *Harmony Hotel* (Warner Bros.,
    93).

**Don't Tear Me Up** (English)
Words and music by Mick Jagger.
Promopub B. V., CH-1017 Amsterdam, Netherlands, 1992.
Best-selling record by Mick Jagger from *Wandering Spirit* (Atlantic,
    93).

**Don't Walk Away**
Words and music by Vassal Benford and Ron Spearman.
Gradington Music, 1992/MCA Music, 1992/Ronnie Onyx, 1992.
Best-selling record by Jade from *Jade to the Max* (Giant/Reprise, 93).

**Down with the King**
Words and music by Joseph Simmons, Darryl McDaniels, Pete Phillips,
    John Penn, James Rado, Gerome Ragni, and Galt Mcdermott.
Protoons Inc., 1993/Rush Groove, 1993/Smooth Flowin', 1993/Pete
    Rock, 1993/EMI U Catalogue.
Best-selling record by Run D.M.C. from *Down with the King* (Profile,
    93).

**Dre Day**
Words and music by Dr. Dre (pseudonym for Andre Young), Snoop
    (pseudonym for Calvin Broadus), and Colin Wolfe.
Ain't Nothin' Goin on But Fu-kin, 1992.
Best-selling record by Dr. Dre from *The Chronic* (Death Row/
    Interscope/Priority, 92).

**Dreamlover**
Words and music by Mariah Carey and Dave Hall.
Rye Songs, 1993/Sony Songs, 1993/Stone Jam Music, 1993/Ness, Nitty
    & Capone, 1993.
Best-selling record by Mariah Carey from *Music Box* (Columbia, 93).

**Dreams** (English)
Words and music by Gabrielle.
Perfect, 1993/CPZ, 1993/Zomba Music, 1993.

Best-selling record by Gabrielle from *Find Your Way* (Go! Discs/ London, 93).

**Drive South**
Words and music by John Hiatt.
Lillybilly, 1988/Bug Music, 1988.
Revived by Suzy Bogguss from *Voices in the Wind* (Liberty, 92).

# E

**Easy** (English)
Words and music by Polly Jean Harvey.
Hot Head Ltd. (England), 1992.
Introduced by P.J. Harvey on *4-Track Demos* (Island, 93).

**Easy Come, Easy Go**
Words and music by Aaron Barker and Dean Dillon.
O-Tex Music, 1993/Acuff Rose Music, 1993.
Best-selling record by George Strait on *Easy Come, Easy Go* (MCA, 93).

**Eat the Music** (English)
Words and music by Kate Bush.
Kate Bush Music, Ltd., London, England, 1993.
Introduced by Kate Bush on *The Red Shoes* (Columbia, 93).

**Effigy**
Words and music by John Fogerty.
Jondora Music, 1969.
Revived by Uncle Tupelo on *No Alternative* (Arista, 93). An old
Credence Clear water Revival tune. Album is a compilation
benefitting AIDS research.

**88 Lines About 44 Women**
Words and music by David Kaufman.
City Beat Music, 1981.
Revived by The Nails on *Living in Oblivion II* (EMI, 93). Previously
available on *Hotel for Women* (81) and *Mood Swing* (84).

**Eileen** (English)
Words and music by Keith Richards and Steve Jordan.
Promopub B. V., CH-1017 Amsterdam, Netherlands, 1992/Warner-
Tamerlane Music, 1992/Risque Situe Music, 1992.
Introduced by Keith Richards on *Main Offender* (Virgin, 92).

**Empty Promises**
Words and music by Kristen Hall.
Ludakris, 1992/BMG Music, 1992.
Introduced by Kristen Hall on *Fact & Fiction* (High Street, 92).

**English Boy** (English)
Words and music by Peter Townshend.
Eel Pie Music, 1993/Towser Tunes Inc., 1993.
Introduced by Pete Townshend in *Psycho Derelict* (Atlanta, 93).

**Even Here We Are**
Words and music by Paul Westerberg.
Elegant Mule, 1993.
Introduced by Paul Westerberg on *14 Songs* (Sire/Reprise, 93).

**Even Then** (Netherlands)
Music by Ad van Dijk, Dutch words by Koen van Dijk, English words
    by Peter Reeves and Sheldon Harnick.
Introduced by Anne Renolfsson in *Cyrano* (93). Musical originated in
    Holland.

**Every Little Thing**
Words and music by Carlene Carter and Al Anderson.
Sony Cross Keys Publishing Co. Inc., 1993/Tortured Artist, 1993/Bash,
    1993/This Big, 1993.
Best-selling record by Carlene Carter from *Little Love Letters* (Giant,
    93).

**Everybody Hurts**
Words and music by William Berry, Peter Buck, Mike Mills, and
    Michael Stipe.
Night Garden Music, 1993/Unichappell Music Inc., 1993.
Best-selling record by R.E.M. on *Automatic for the People*.

**Everybody Lay Down**
Words and music by Pat Geraldo and Neil Geraldo.
Spyder Mae, 1993/Big Tooth Music Corp., 1993/Chrysalis Music Group,
    1993.
Introduced by Pat Benatar on *Gravity's Rainbow* (Chrysalis/EMI, 93).

**Everything Comes Down to Money and Love**
Words and music by Dave Loggins and Gove Scrivener.
MCA Music, 1993/Emerald River, 1993/Music of the World, 1993.
Introduced by Hank Williams, Jr. on *Out of Control* (Capricorn, 93).

**Everything in the World** (English)
Words and music by Chris Difford and Glenn Tilbrook.
EMI-Virgin, 1993.
Introduced by Squeeze on *Some Fantastic Place* (A&M, 93).

**Everything's Gonna Be Alright**
Words and music by Father M.C., Mark Morales, Mark Rooney, and
   Daron Johnson.
EMI-April Music, 1992/Across 110th Street Music, 1993/Father MC,
   1993/Music of the World, 1993/Second Generation Rooney Tunes,
   1993/EMI-Blackwood Music Inc., 1993/Flow Tech, 1993.
Best-selling record by Father M.C. from *Close to You* (Uptown/MCA,
   92).

**Eyes That Never Lie**
Music by Alan Menken, words by David Spencer.
Trunksong Music, 1993.
Introduced by Sal Viviano in the musical *The Girl Who Was Plugged In*
   (93). Also on the album *Weird Romance* (Columbia, 93).

# F

**Fast As You**
Words and music by Dwight Yoakam.
Coal Dust West, 1993/Warner-Tamerlane Music, 1993.
Best-selling record by Dwight Yoakam from *This Time* (Reprise, 93).

**Feed the Tree**
Words and music by Tanya Donelly.
Slow Dog Music, 1993.
Introduced by Belly on *Star* (Sire/Reprise, 93). Alternative stars recall
the Bangles.

**Feel Like Falling**
Words and music by Wally Wilson and Ashley Cleveland.
Sony Cross Keys Publishing Co. Inc., 1993/Warner-Tamerlane Music,
1993.
Introduced by Ashley Cleveland on *Bus Named Desire*.

**Fields of Gold** (English)
Words and music by Sting (pseudonym for Gordon Sumner).
Blue Turtle, 1993.
Best-selling record by Sting from *Ten Summoner's Tales* (A&M, 93).

**Fields of Gray**
Words and music by Bruce Hornsby.
WB Music, 1993/Basically Zappo Music, 1993.
Introduced by Bruce Hornsby on *Harbor Lights* (RCA, 93).

**50 Ft. Queenie** (English)
Words and music by Polly Jean Harvey.
Hot Head Ltd. (England), 1993.
Introduced by P.J. Harvey on *Rid of Me* (Island, 93).

**Fireman's Wedding**
Words and music by Joe Henry.
Sony Cross Keys Publishing Co. Inc., 1993.
Introduced by Joe Henry on *Kindness of the World* (Mammoth, 93).

**Forever in Love**
Words and music by Kenny Gurewitz.
Kenny G, 1993.
Best-selling record by Kenny G. from *Breathless* (Arista, 93).

**Found out About You**
Words and music by Doug Hopkins.
WB Music, 1992/East Jesus, 1993.
Introduced by Gin Blossoms on *New Miserable Experience* (A&M, 92).
Songwriter Hopkins committed suicide while this song was moving up the charts.

**Fragile** (English)
Words and music by Sting (pseudonym for Gordon Sumner).
Blue Turtle, 1987.
Revived by Dionne Warwick on *Friends Can Be Lovers* (Arista, 93). A big year for Sting; a fizzled comeback for Warwick.

**Freak Me**
Words and music by Keith Sweat and Roy Murray.
Keith Sweat Music, 1992/E/A Music, 1992/WB Music, 1992/Saints Alive, 1992.
Best-selling record by Silk from *Lose Control* (Keia/Elektra, 92).

**Free Your Mind**
Words and music by Thom McElroy and Denzil Foster.
Irving Music Inc., 1992.
Best-selling record by En Vogue from *Funky Divas* (Atco/EastWest, 92). A strong message from the otherwise frilly pop group.

**Friend Like Me**
Music by Alan Menken, words by Howard Ashman.
Walt Disney Music, 1992/Wonderland Music, 1992.
Introduced in the film and soundtrack of *Aladdin* (Walt Disney, 92).
Nominated for a Grammy Award, Best movie or TV Song of the Year, 1993.

**Friends to the End**
Words by Leslee Bricusse, music by Henry Mancini.
RET Music Inc., 1993.
Introduced by Tom and Jerry in the film *Tom and Jerry* (93).

# G

**Gangsta**
Words and music by Dr. Freeze (pseudonym for Louis Freese).
Hi-Frost, 1993/Hip City, 1993.
Best-selling record by Bell Biv Devoe on *Hootie Mack* (Motown, 93).

**Gangsta Lean**
Words and music by Chris Jackson, E. Jay Turner, and Tracy Carter.
Rap and More Music, 1993.
Best-selling record by DRS on *51* (Capitol, 93). Poetic depiction of life
  in the ghetto.

**Gepetto**
Words and music by Tanya Donelly.
Slow Dog Music, 1993.
Introduced by Belly on *Star* (Sire/Reprise, 93).

**Get a Haircut**
Words and music by David Avery and Bill Birch.
Champaign House, 1993/Del Sounds Music, 1993.
Best-selling record by George Thorogood from *Haircut* (EMI, 93).

**Get Away**
Words and music by Teddy Riley, Bernard Belle, Tony Haynes, and
  Bobby Brown.
Zomba Music, 1992/Donril Music, 1992/WB Music, 1992/B. Funk,
  1992/Polygram International, 1992/Toe Knee Hangs, 1992/MCA
  Music, 1992/Bobby Brown, 1992.
Best-selling record by Bobby Brown from *Bobby* (MCA, 92).

**Get out of Control** (English)
Words and music by Daniel Ash.
Momentum Ltd., 1992/WB Music, 1992/Beggar's Banquet, 1992.
Best-selling record by Daniel Ash from *Foolish Thing Desire*
  (Columbia, 92).

**Getto Jam**
Words and music by Domino and Kevin Gilliam.
No Dooze, 1993/Cats on the Prowl, 1993.
Best-selling record by Domino from *Domino* (RAL/Chaos, 93).

**Girl, I've Been Hurt** (Canadian)
Words and music by Darrin O'Brien, Shawn Moltke, and Edmond
    Leary.
Motor Jam, 1993/Green Snow, 1993/M.C. Shan, 1993/WB Music, 1993.
Best-selling record by Snow from *12 Inches of Snow* (EastWest, 93).

**Girl U for Me/Lose Control**
Words and music by Keith Sweat and Roy Murray.
Keith Sweat Music, 1993/E/A Music, 1993/Warner-Tamerlane Music,
    1993/Saints Alive, 1993/EMI-Blackwood Music Inc., 1993.
Best-selling record by Silk from *Lose Control* (K E I A/Elektra, 93).

**Give It All Away** (English)
Words and music by Karl Wallinger.
Polygram International, 1993.
Introduced by Karl Wallinger on *Bong* (Chrysalis, 93).

**Give It up, Turn It Loose**
Words and music by Thom McElroy and Denzil Foster.
Two Tuff-Enuff Music, 1992/Irving Music Inc., 1992.
Best-selling record by En Vogue from *Funky Divas* (A&CO EastWest,
    92).

**Go**
Words and music by Pearl Jam.
Innocent Bystander Music, 1993/Write Treatage Music, 1993/Scribing
    C-Ment Music, 1993/Pickled Fish Music, 1993/Jumping Cat Music,
    1993.
Best-selling record by Pearl Jam on *Vs* (Epic, 93).

**Got No Shame**
Words and music by Daron Johnson and Marti Frederiksen.
EMI-Virgin, 1993/Heathalee, 1993/Pearl White, 1993.
Best-selling record by Brother Cane from *Brother Cane* (Virgin, 93).

**The Grand Tour**
Words and music by George Richey, Carmol Taylor, and Norro Wilson.
Al Gallico Music Corp., 1974/Algee Music Corp., 1974.
Revived by Aaron Neville on *The Grand Tour* (A&M, 93).

# H

**Had It, Done It, Been There, Did That**
Words and music by Mike Walsh.
Warner-Tamerlane Music, 1993.
Introduced by Mike Walsh (Imago, 93). New rallying cry for the numb
  nineties.

**Hang onto Your Ego**
Words and music by Brian Wilson.
Rondor Music Inc., 1966.
Revived by Frank Black on *Frank Black* (4AD/Elektra, 93).

**Harbor Lights**
Words and music by Bruce Hornsby.
WB Music, 1993/Basically Zappo Music, 1993.
Introduced by Bruce Hornsby in *Harbor Lights* (RCA, 93).

**The Hard Way**
Words and music by Mary-Chapin Carpenter.
Getarealjob Music, 1992/EMI-April Music, 1993.
Best-selling record by Mary Chapin-Carpenter from *Come on, Come on*
  (Columbia, 92). Nominated for a Grammy Award, Country Song of
  the Year, 1993.

**Harts of the West**
Words and music by Clint Black.
Blackened, 1993.
Introduced by Clint Black as theme for the TV show *Harts of the West*.

**Harvest Moon**
Words and music by Neil Young.
Silver Fiddle, 1992.
Introduced by Neil Young on *Harvest Moon* (Reprise, 92). Nominated
  for Grammy Awards, Record of the Year, 1993, and Song of the
  Year, 1993.

**Hat 2 Da Back**
Words and music by Dallas Austin, Lisa Lopes, and Kevin Wales.
EMI Music Publishing, 1992/D.A.R.P. Music, 1992/Longitude Music, 1992.
Best-selling record by TLC from *Oooooooohhh...On the TLC Tip* (LaFace/Arista, 92).

**Hatred (A Duet)** (English)
Words and music by Ray Davies.
Davray Music, Ltd., London, England, 1993.
Introduced by The Kinks on *Phobia* (Columbia, 93).

**Have I Told You Lately**
Words and music by Van Morrison.
Essential Music, 1989/Rightsong Music, 1989.
Revived by Rod Stewart from *Unplugged and Seated* (Warner Bros., 93).

**Heal the World**
Words and music by Michael Jackson.
Mijac Music, 1992/Warner-Tamerlane Music, 1992/Hudmar Publishing Co., Inc., 1992.
Best-selling record by Michael Jackson from *Dangerous* (Epic, 92).

**Heart Shaped Box**
Words and music by Nirvana.
End of Music, 1993/Virgin Songs, 1993.
Introduced by Nirvana on *In Utero* (DGC, 93).

**The Heart Won't Lie**
Words and music by Kim Carnes and Donna Weiss.
Moonwindow Music, 1993/Donna Weiss Music, 1993.
Best-selling record by Reba McEntire and Vince Gill from *It's Your Call* (MCA, 92). Song was performed on the TV series *Evening Shade*.

**Heartbeats Accelerating** (Canadian)
Words and music by Kate McGarrigle.
Garden Court Music Co., 1990.
Revived by Linda Ronstadt on *Winter Light* (Elektra, 93).

**Heartland**
Words and music by Steve Dorff and John Bettis.
Warner-Tamerlane Music, 1992/Nocturnal Eclipse Music, 1992/WB Music, 1992/John Bettis Music, 1992.
Best-selling record by George Strait from the film and soundtrack album *Pure Country* (MCA, 92).

**Heartland**
Words and music by Willie Nelson and Bob Dylan.
Special Rider Music, 1992/Act Five, 1992.
Introduced by Willie Nelson with Bob Dylan on *Across the Borderline* (Columbia, 93).

**Hearts Are Gonna Roll**
Words and music by Hal Ketchum and Ronnie Scaife.
Foreshadow Songs, Inc., 1992/Songs of Polygram, 1992/Virgin Timber, 1992.
Best-selling record by Hal Ketchum from *Sure Love* (Curb, 92).

**Heaven Knows**
Words and music by Luther Vandross.
EMI-April Music, 1993/Uncle Ronnie's Music, 1993.
Introduced by Luther Vandross on *Never Let Me Go* (Epic, 93).
   Nominated for a Grammy Award, Best R&B Song of the Year, 1993.

**Heaven's Just a Sin Away**
Words and music by Jerry Gillespie.
Blue Lake Music, 1977.
Revived by Kelly Willis on *Kelly Willis*.

**Here We Go Again**
Words and music by Michael Angelo Saulsbury, Eric Kirkland, Phillip Johnson, Stevie Wonder, and Susaye Green.
Hee Bee Dooinit, 1992/Unit 4, 1992/WB Music, 1992/Stone Diamond Music, 1992/Jobete Music Co., Inc., 1992/Black Bull Music, 1992/Doll Face, 1992.
Best-selling record by Portrait from *Portrait* (Capitol, 92).

**Hero** (English)
Words and music by Phil Collins and David Crosby.
Hidden Pun, 1993/Hit & Run Music, 1993/Phil Collins, 1993/Stay Straight, 1993.
Introduced by David Crosby on *A Thousand Roads* (Atlantic, 93).

**Hero**
Words and music by Walter Afanasieff and Mariah Carey.
Sony Songs, 1993/Rye Songs, 1993/WB Music, 1993/Wallyworld Music, 1993.
Best-selling record by Mariah Carey from *Music Box* (Columbia, 93).

**Heroin**
Words and music by Lou Reed.
Oakfield Avenue Music Ltd., 1967/Screen Gems-EMI Music Inc., 1967.
Revived by Billy Idol on *Cyberpunk* (Chrysalis/ERG, 93).

**Hey Jealousy**
Words and music by Doug Hopkins.
WB Music, 1992/East Jesus, 1992.
Best-selling record by Gin Blossoms from *New Miserable Experience*
  (A&M, 92).

**Hey Mr. DJ**
Words and music by Kier Gist, Vincent Brown, Anthony Criss, Renee
  Andrea Neufville, Arthur Bahr, Leon Ware, and Zane Grey.
Naughty, 1993/T-Boy Music Publishing Co., Inc., 1993/Flavor Unit
  Music, 1993/Almo Music Corp., 1993/Irving Music Inc., 1993/O/B/O/
  Itself, 1993/Medad, 1993.
Best-selling record by Zhane from *Roll with the Flava* (Flava, 93).

**Highway 61 Revisited**
Words and music by Bob Dylan.
Special Rider Music, 1965.
Revived by PJ Harvey on *Rid of Me* (Island, 93).

**Hip Hop Hooray**
Words and music by Naughty by Nature.
T-Boy Music Publishing Co., Inc., 1992/Naughty, 1992.
Best-selling record by Naughty by Nature from *19 Naughty III* (Tommy
  Boy, 93).

**Holdin' Heaven**
Words and music by Bill Kenner and Thom McHugh.
Tom Collins Music Corp., 1993/Music of the World, 1993.
Best-selling record by Tracy Byrd from *Tracy Byrd* (MCA, 93).

**Hometown Honeymoon**
Words and music by John Lee and Jim Photoglo.
Warner/Elektra/Asylum Music, 1992/Mopage, 1992/After Berger, 1992/
  Patrix Janus, 1992/WB Music, 1992.
Best-selling record by Alabama from *American Pride* (RCA, 92).

**Hope of Deliverance** (English)
Words and music by Paul McCartney.
MPL Communications Inc., 1993.
Introduced by Paul McCartney on *Off the Ground* (Capitol, 93).

**Hopelessly** (Canadian)
Words and music by Rick Astley and Rob Fisher.
BMG Music, 1993.
Best-selling record by Rick Astley from *Body & Soul* (RCA, 93).

**How Can I Win**
Music by Marvin Hamlisch, words by David Zippel.
Introduced by Bernadette Peters in the musical *Goodbye Girls* (93).

**Human Behaviour** (Swedish)
English words and music by Nellee Hooper and Bjork Gudmundsdottir.
Polygram Music Publishing Inc., 1993/Warner-Chappell Music, 1993.
Best-selling record by Bjork from *Debut* (Elektra, 93).

**Human Wheels**
Words and music by John Mellencamp and George Michael Green.
Windswept Pacific, 1993/Full Keel, 1993/WB Music, 1993/Katsback,
    1993.
Best-selling record by John Mellencamp from *Human Wheels* (Mercury,
    93).

# I

**I Ain't Goin' out Like That**
Words and music by Dr. Freeze (pseudonym for Louis Freese), Larry
  Muggurud, and T. Ray.
BMG Music, 1993/Cypress Phunky, 1993/MCA Music, 1993/Soul
  Assassins Music, 1993/T-Ray, 1993.
Best-selling record by Cypress Hill from *Black Sunday* (Ruffhouse/
  Columbia, 93).

**I Almost Had a Weakness** (English)
Words and music by Elvis Costello (pseudonym for DeClan McManus)
  and Michael Thomas.
Plangent Visions Music, Inc., London, England, 1992.
Introduced by Elvis Costello and the Brodsky Quartet on *The Juliet
  Letters* (Warner Bros., 93).

**I Believe My Own Eyes** (English)
Words and music by Peter Townshend.
Eel Pie Music, 1992.
Introduced by Marcia Mitzman and Jonathan Dokuchitz in the musical
  *Tommy* (RCA, 93).

**I Can See Clearly Now** (Jamaican)
Words and music by Johnny Nash.
Dovan Music, 1972.
Revived by Jimmy Cliff in the film and soundtrack *Cool Runnings*
  (Chaos, 93).

**I Don't Call Him Daddy**
Words and music by Reed Nielsen.
Englishtown, 1993.
Best-selling record by Doug Supernaw from *Red and Rio Grande* (BNA,
  93).

**I Don't Know Why**
Words and music by Shawn Colvin.

AGF Music Ltd., 1992/Scred Songs, 1992.
Introduced by Shawn Colvin on *Fat City* (Columbia, 93).

**I Don't Wanna Fight** (English)
Words and music by Steve Duberry, Lulu, and Billy Lawrie.
Chrysalis Music Group, 1992/Bilv, 1993/Ensign Music, 1993.
Best-selling record by Tina Turner from the film and soundtrack album
*What's Love Got to Do with It* (Virgin, 93). Nominated for a Grammy
Award, Movie or TV Song of the Year, 1993.

**I Feel You** (English)
Words and music by Martin Gore.
Grabbing Hands, 1993/EMI Music Publishing, 1993/EMI-Blackwood
Music Inc., 1993.
Best-selling record by Depeche Mode from *Songs of Faith and Devotion*
(Sire/Reprise, 93).

**I Get Around**
Words and music by Tupac Shakur, Shock-G, Roger Troutman, Lester
Troutman, and S. Murdock.
GLG Two, 1993/Ghetto Gospel, 1993/Rubber Band Music, Inc., 1993/
Saja Music Co., 1993/Troutman's, 1993/Interscope Pearl, 1993/
Warner-Tamerlane Music, 1993.
Best-selling record by 2Pac from *Strictly 4 My N.I.G.G.A.Z.* (Interscope,
93).

**I Got a Man**
Words and music by Positive K.
Step Up Front, 1993.
Best-selling record by Positive K from *Skills Dat Pay Da Bills* (Island,
93).

**I Got No Idols**
Words and music by Juliana Hatfield.
Juliana Hatfield, 1993.
Introduced by The Juliana Hatfield Three on *Become What You Are*
(Mammoth/Atlantic, 93).

**I Have Nothing**
Words and music by David Foster and Linda Thompson.
Warner-Tamerlane Music, 1992/One Four Three, 1992/Linda's Boys
Music, 1992.
Best-selling record by Whitney Houston from the film and soundtrack of
*The Bodyguard* (Arista, 92). Nominated for a Grammy Award, Movie
or TV Song of the Year, 1993.

**I Just Want to See You So Bad**
Words and music by Lucinda Williams.
Lucy Jones Music, 1988/Nomad-Noman, 1988/Warner-Tamerlane

Music, 1988.
Revived by Barrence Whitfield with Tom Russell on *Hillbilly Voodoo* (East Side Digital, 93).

**I Love the Way You Love Me**
Words and music by Victoria Shaw and Chuck Cannon.
Gary Morris Music, 1992/Taste Auction, 1992.
Best-selling record by John Michael Montgomery from *Life's a Dance* (Atlantic, 92).

**I Will Always Love You**
Words and music by Dolly Parton.
Velvet Apple Music, 1973.
Best-selling record by Whitney Houston from the film and soundtrack of *The Bodyguard* (Arista, 92). Song became the longest running number-one tune in pop history. Won a Grammy Award,      Record of the year, 1993.

**I Will Find You** (Irish)
Words and music by Ciaran Brennan.
Clannad Music Ltd. (Ireland), 1992/BMG Music, 1993.
Introduced by Clannad on *Banta* (Atlantic, 93). Used as the theme for the movie *The Last of the Mohicans* (93).

**I Wouldn't Normally Do This Kind of Thing** (English)
Words and music by Neil Tennant and Chris Lowe.
EMI-Virgin, 1993.
Introduced by Pet Shop Boys on *Very* (Erg/EMI, 93).

**I'd Do Anything for Love (But I Won't Do That)**
Words and music by Jim Steinman.
E. B. Marks Music Corp., 1993.
Best-selling record by Meat Loaf on *Bat Out of Hell II: Back into Hell* (MCA, 93). Massive return to form for songwriter Steinman and his beefy pal. Nominated for Grammy Awards, Rock Song of the Year, 1993, and Song of the Year, 1993.

**If**
Words and music by Janet Jackson, James Harris, III, and Terry Lewis.
Black Ice Music, 1993/Flyte Tyme Tunes, 1993/Jobete Music Co., Inc., 1993/Stone Agate Music, 1993.
Best-selling record by Janet Jackson from *janet* (Virgin, 93).

**If I Ever Lose My Faith In You** (English)
Words and music by Sting (pseudonym for Gordon Sumner).
Blue Turtle, 1993.
Best-selling record by Sting from *Ten Summoner's Tales* (A&M, 93) Nominated for Grammy Awards, Record of the Year, 1993, and Song of the Year, 1993.

**If I Had No Loot**
Words and music by Raphael Wiggins, J. Bautista, Will Harris, and
O'Shea Jackson.
Polygram International, 1993/Tony! Toni! Tone!, 1993/Gangsta Boogie,
1993/Big Will, 1993/Street Knowledge, 1993/Ghatti Music, 1993/L.A.
Jay, 1993/WB Music, 1993.
Best-selling record by Tony! Toni! Tone! from *Sons of Soul* (Wing/
Mercury, 93).

**I'll Never Get over You (Getting over Me)**
Words and music by Diane Warren.
Realsongs, 1992.
Best-selling record by Expose from *Expose* (Arista, 93).

**I'm Alive**
Words and music by Jackson Browne.
Swallow Turn Music, 1993.
Introduced by Jackson Browne on *I'm Alive* (Elektra, 93).

**I'm Every Woman**
Words and music by Nick Ashford and Valerie Simpson.
Nick-O-Val Music, 1978.
Revived by Whitney Houston in the film and soundtrack for *The
Bodyguard* (Arista, 92).Formerly a hit by Chaka Kahn.

**I'm Free**
Words and music by Jon Secada and Miguel Morejon.
Estefan Music, 1992.
Best-selling record by Jon Secada from *Jon Secada* (SBK/ERG, 92).

**I'm Gonna Be (500 Miles)** (Scottish)
Words and music by Craig Reid and Charlie Reid.
Warner-Chappell Music, 1988/Warner-Tamerlane Music.
Revived by The Proclaimers in the film and soundtrack album *Benny
and Joon* (Chrysalis, 93) and on *Sunshine on Leith* (Chrysalis, 93).

**I'm So into You**
Words and music by Brian Alexander Morgan.
Bam Jams, 1993/Warner-Tamerlane Music, 1993/Interscope Pearl, 1993.
Best-selling record by SWV from *It's About Time* (RCA, 93).

**I'm the Only One**
Words and music by Melissa Etheridge.
MLE Music, 1993/Almo Music Corp., 1993.
Introduced by Melissa Etheridge on *Yes I Am* (Island, 93).

**In a Week or Two**
Words and music by Jerry House and Gary Burr.
Madwoman, 1992/MCA Music, 1992/Gary Burr Music, 1992/Sony Tree,

1992.
Best-selling record by Diamond Rio from *Close to the Edge* (Arista, 92).

**In All the Right Places** (English)
Words and music by John Barry, Lisa Stansfield, Ian Devaney, and Andy Morris.
Big Life Music, 1993/Careers-BMG, 1993.
Introduced by Lisa Stansfield in the film and soundtrack album *Indecent Proposal* (MCA, 93).

**In the Heart of a Woman**
Words and music by Keith Hinton and Brett Cartwright.
WB Music, 1993/Warner-Tamerlane Music, 1993/Brupo, 1993.
Best-selling record by Billy Ray Cyrus from *It Won't Be the Last* (Mercury, 93).

**In These Arms**
Words and music by Jon Bon Jovi, Richie Sambora, and Dave Bryan.
Polygram International, 1992/Bon Jovi Publishing, 1992/Aggressive, 1992/Moon Junction, 1992/EMI-April Music, 1992.
Best-selling record by Bon Jovi from *Keep the Faith* (Jambco/Mercury, 92).

**Infamous Angel**
Words and music by Iris DeMent.
Forerunner Music, 1993/Songs of Iris, 1993.
Introduced by Iris DeMent in *Infamous Angel* (WB, 93).

**Informer** (Canadian)
Words and music by Darrin O'Brien, Shawn Moltke, and Edmond Leary.
Motor Jam, 1993/Green Snow, 1993/M.C. Shan, 1993.
Best-selling record by Snow from *12 Inches of Snow* (Atco EastWest, 93). The year's crossover reggae sensation.

**Insane in the Brain**
Words and music by Dr. Freeze (pseudonym for Louis Freese), Senen Reyes, and Larry Muggurud.
Cypress Phunky, 1993/Soul Assassins Music, 1993/MCA Music, 1993/BMG Music, 1993.
Best-selling record by Cypress Hill from *Black Sunday* (Ruffhouse/Columbia, 93). Celebrating a reefer resurgence.

**Into Your Arms**
Words and music by Robin St. Clare.
Polygram Music Publishing Inc., 1993/Moo Music, 1993.
Best-selling record by the Lemonheads from *Come on Feel* (Atlantic, 93). Sophomore year for the college-audience sensations.

**Is It Like Today** (English)
Words and music by Karl Wallinger.
Polygram International, 1993.
Introduced by Karl Wallinger on *Bong* (Ensign/Chrysalis/Erg, 93).

**It Sure Is Monday**
Words and music by Dennis Linde.
EMI-Blackwood Music Inc., 1993/Linde Manor Publishing Co., 1993.
Best-selling record by Mark Chesnutt from *Almost Goodbye* (MCA, 93).

**It Was a Good Day**
Words and music by Ice Cube.
Gangsta Boogie, 1992/WB Music, 1992.
Best-selling record by Ice Cube from *The Predator* (Priority, 92).

**It's a Hard Life Wherever You Go**
Words and music by Nanci Griffith.
Irving Music Inc., 1989/Ponder Heart Music, 1989.
Revived by Nanci Griffith (Elektra, 93).

**It's a Little Too Late**
Words and music by Pat Terry and Roger Murrah.
Castle Street, 1992/End of August, 1992/Murrah, 1992.
Best-selling record by Tanya Tucker from *Can't Run from Yourself* (Liberty, 92).

**It's All in the Heart**
Words and music by Stephanie Davis.
EMI-Blackwood Music Inc., 1993/Beartooth Music, 1993.
Best-selling record by Stephanie Davis from *Stephanie Davis* (Asylum, 93).

**It's for You**
Words and music by Shanice Wilson, Michael Angelo Saulsbury, and Eric Kirkland.
Shanice 4U, 1993/Hee Bee Dooinit, 1993/WB Music, 1993/U/A Music, Inc., 1993.
Introduced by Shanice in the film and soundtrack album *Meteor Man* (Motown, 93).

**It's Gonna Be a Lovely Day**
Words and music by Bill Withers, Skip Scarborough, Rob Clivilles, David Cole, Tommy Never, and Michele Visage.
Unichappell Music Inc., 1991/Golden Withers, 1991.
Best-selling record by the S.O.U.L S.Y.S.T.E.M. from the film and soundtrack of *The Bodyguard* (Arista, 92). Featured on the album *Anything Goes* (Arista, 93).

# J

**Jessie**
Words and music by Joshua Kadison.
Joshuasongs, 1993/Seymour Glass, 1993/EMI-Blackwood Music Inc.,
   1993.
Best-selling record by Josh Kadison on *Painted Desert Serenade* (SBK,
   93).

**Just Kickin' It**
Words and music by Jermaine Dupri and Manuel Seals.
So So Def Music, 1993/EMI-April Music, 1993/Full Keel, 1993/Ground
   Control, 1993.
Best-selling record by Xscape from *Hummin' Comin' at Cha'* (So So
   Def/Columbia, 93).

**Just Like Always**
Words and music by Jimmy Webb.
White Oak Songs, 1993.
Introduced by Jimmy Webb on *Suspending Disbelief* (Elektra, 93).

# K

**Keep Ya Head Up**
Words and music by Tupac Shakur, Darrell Anderson, and Roger
    Troutman.
Ghetto Gospel, 1993/Interscope Pearl, 1993/Warner-Tamerlane Music,
    1993/Rubber Band Music, Inc., 1993.
Best-selling record by 2Pac from *Strictly 4 My N.I.G.G.A.Z.* (Interscope,
    93)

**Knockin' Da Boots**
Words and music by Shazam, Dino Conner, Stick (pseudonym for
    Bishop Burrell), and Roger Troutman.
Pac Jam Publishing, 1992/Saja Music Co., 1992/Troutman's, 1992.
Best-selling record by H-Town from *Fever for Da Flavor* (Luke, 93).

# L

**Lately**
Words and music by Stevie Wonder.
Jobete Music Co., Inc., 1980/Black Bull Music, 1980.
Revived by Jodeci from *Uptown MTV Unplugged* (Uptown, 93).

**Learning to Live Again**
Words and music by Stephanie Davis and Don Schlitz.
EMI-Blackwood Music Inc., 1992/Beartooth Music, 1992/Don Schlitz
    Music, 1992/Almo Music Corp., 1992.
Best-selling record by Garth Brooks from *The Chase* (Liberty, 92).

**Leave It to the Girls**
Words and music by Charles Strouse and Martin Charnin.
MPL Communications Inc., 1991.
Introduced by Donna McKechnie and Alene Robertson in *Annie
    Warbucks* (93). Newly revived sequel to *Annie*.

**Lemon** (Irish)
Words and music by Bono, words and music by U2.
Polygram International, 1993.
Introduced by U2 on *Zooropa* (Island, 93).

**Let Me Ride**
Words and music by Dr. Dre (pseudonym for Andre Young) and Snoop
    (pseudonym for Calvin Broadus).
Sony Tunes, 1992.
Best-selling record by Dr. Dre on *The Chronic* (Death Row/Interscope/
    Priority, 93).

**The Letter Home** (English)
Words and music by Elvis Costello (pseudonym for DeClan McManus),
    music by Ian Belton, words by Paul Cassidy.
Plangent Visions Music, Inc., London, England, 1992.
Introduced by Elvis Costello and the Brodsky Quartet on *The Juliet
    Letters* (Warner Bros., 93).

**Lines Around Your Eyes**
Words and music by Lucinda Williams.
Lucy Jones Music, 1992/Nomad-Noman, 1992/Warner-Tamerlane
   Music, 1992.
Introduced by Lucinda Williams on *Sweet Old World* (Chameleon, 92).

**Linger** (Irish)
Words and music by Noel Hogan and Dolores O'Riordan.
Island Music, 1993/Polygram International, 1993.
Best-selling record by The Cranberries from *Everybody Else Is Doing It,
   So Why Can't We?* (Island, 93).

**Little Miracles (Happen Every Day)**
Words and music by Luther Vandross and Marcus Miller.
EMI-April Music, 1993/Uncle Ronnie's Music, 1993/Thriller Miller
   Music, 1993/MCA Music, 1993.
Introduced by Luther Vandross on *Never Let Me Go* (Epic, 93).
   Nominated for a Grammy Award, Best R&B Song of the Year, 1993.

**Little Victories**
Words and music by Darden Smith.
Crooked Fingers, 1993/AGF Music Ltd., 1993.
Introduced by Darden Smith on *Little Victories* (Chaos/Columbia, 93).

**Livin' on the Edge**
Words and music by Steven Tyler, Joe Perry, and Mark Hudson.
Swag Song Music, 1993/MCA Music, 1993/Beef Puppet, 1993.
Best-selling record by Aerosmith from *Get a Grip* (Geffen, 93).
   Nominated for a Grammy Award, Rock Song of the Year, 1993.

**Living the Blues**
Words and music by Tracy Nelson and Gary Nicholson.
Rose Hips Music, 1993/Sony Cross Keys Publishing Co. Inc., 1993.
Introduced by Tracy Nelson on *In the Here and Now* (Rounder, 93).

**London's Brilliant** (English)
Words and music by Elvis Costello (pseudonym for DeClan McManus)
   and Caitlin O'Riordan.
Plangent Visions Music, Inc., London, England, 1993.
Introduced by Wendy James on *Now Ain't the Time for Your Tears*
   (MCA, 93).

**Look Heart, No Hands**
Words and music by Trey Bruce and Russell Smith.
MCA Music, 1992.
Best-selling record by Randy Travis from *Greatest Hits, Vol. 2* (Warner
   Bros., 92).

**Lookin' for a Kiss**
Words and music by Johnny Thunders and David Johansen.
Seldak Music Corp., 1974/Haverstraw, 1974.
Revived by Jayne County on *Goddess of Wet Dreams* (ESP, 93).
  Bringing back a trashy epic from the N.Y. Dolls.

**Looking Through Patient Eyes**
Words and music by Atrel Cordes and George Michael.
MCA Music, 1992.
Best-selling record by P.M. Dawn from *The Bliss Album...?* (Gee Street/
  Island, 93).

**Loser**
Words and music by Beck Hansen and Karl Stephenson.
BMG Songs Inc., 1992/Fluxin Music, 1992.
Introduced by Beck (Bongload, 93). As 1993 closed, the subject of a
  record label bidding war; won by Geffen, which released it on the
  album *Mellow Gold.*

**Love Can Move Mountains**
Words and music by Diane Warren.
Realsongs, 1992.
Best-selling record by Celine Dion from *Celine Dion* (Epic, 92).

**Love Don't Love You**
Words and music by Thom McElroy and Denzil Foster.
Two Tuff-Enuff Music, 1992/Irving Music Inc., 1992.
Best-selling record by En Vogue from *Funky Divas* (EastWest, 92).

**Love Is**
Words and music by Tonio K. (pseudonym for Steve Krikorian) and
  John Keller.
WB Music, 1992/Pressmancherry, 1992/NYM, 1992/Warner-Tamerlane
  Music, 1992/Pressmancherryblossom, 1992/Chekerman, 1992.
Best-selling record by Vanessa Williams and Brian McKnight from the
  TV show and soundtrack album *Beverly Hills 90210* (Giant, 92).

**Love Is Everything** (Canadian)
Words and music by Jane Siberry.
Wing It, 1993/Bug Music, 1993.
Introduced by Jane Siberry on *When I Was a Boy* (Reprise, 93).

**Love Is the Language**
Words and music by David Williams, Marvin Etzioni, Andrew
  Williams, and Val Kilmer.
PSO Ltd., 1993/Sky Garden Music, 1993/Prophet Sharing Music, 1993/
  Famous Music Corp., 1993/Blue Saint Music, 1993.
Introduced by The Williams Brothers on *Harmony Hotel* (Warner Bros.,
  93).

**Love on the Loose, Heart on the Run**
Words and music by Kostas and Anna Lisa Graham.
Songs of Polygram, 1993/Millhouse Music, 1993.
Best-selling record by McBride and the Ride from *Hurry Sundown*
(MCA, 93).

**Love Shoulda Brought You Home**
Words and music by Bo Watson, Babyface (pseudonym for Kenny
Edmunds), and Daryl Simmons.
Saba Seven Music, 1992/Kear Music, 1992/Ensign Music, 1992/Green
Skirt Music, 1992.
Best-selling record by Toni Braxton from the film and soundtrack album
*Boomerang* (Arista, 92).

**Love U More**
Words and music by Sunscreem.
BMG Songs Inc., 1992.
Best-selling record by Sunscreem from *Q3* (Columbia, 92).

**The Lovers That Never Were** (English)
Words and music by Paul McCartney and Elvis Costello (pseudonym
for DeClan McManus).
Plangent Visions Music, Inc., London, England, 1993/MPL
Communications Inc., 1993.
Introduced by Paul McCartney on *Off the Ground* (Capitol, 93).

**Lovin' Arms**
Words and music by Darden Smith.
Crooked Fingers, 1992/AGF Music Ltd., 1992.
Best-selling record by Darden Smith on *Little Victories* (Chaos/
Columbia, 93).

# M

**The Madison County Waltz**
Words and music by Robert James Waller.
Robert James Waller, 1993.
Introduced by Robert James Waller on *The Ballads of Madison County* (Atlantic, 93). Based on the best-selling novel, by its author.

**Man on the Moon**
Words and music by William Berry, Peter Buck, Mike Mills, and Michael Stipe.
Night Garden Music, 1993/Unichappell Music Inc., 1993.
Best-selling record by R.E.M. from *Automatic for the People* (Warner Bros., 92).

**Marble Halls** (Irish)
Words and music by Enya and Nicky Ryan.
SBK Songs, 1993/EMI-Blackwood Music Inc., 1993.
Introduced by Enya on *Shepherd Moons* (Reprise, 93). Featured in the film *The Age of Innocence* (93).

**Maria's Wedding**
Words and music by Larry Kirwan.
Starry Plough Music, 1992.
Introduced by Black 47 on *Fire of Freedom* (SBK, 93).

**Marilyn Monroe** (English)
Words and music by Willie Russell.
Introduced in America by Stephanie Lawrence in *Blood Brothers* (93).

**Mary Jane's Last Dance**
Words and music by Tom Petty.
Gone Gator Music, 1993.
Best-selling record by Tom Petty & The Heartbreakers on *Greatest Hits* (MCA, 93).

**Mercury Blues**
Words and music by Robert Geddins and K.C. Douglas.

B-Flat Publishing Co., 1992/Tradition Music Co., 1992/Bug Music, 1992.
Best-selling record by Alan Jackson from *A Lot About Livin' (and a Little 'Bout Love)* (Arista, 92).

**Mercy Street** (English)
Words and music by Peter Gabriel.
Hidden Music, 1986/Cliofine, 1986.
Revived by Black Uhuru on *Mystical Truth* (Mesa, 93). Introduced by Peter Gabriel on his album *So*.

**Metal Mickey** (English)
Words and music by Brett Anderson and Bernard Butler.
Polygram International, 1993.
Introduced by Suede on *Suede* (Nude/Columbia, 93).

**A Minor Variation**
Words and music by Billy Joel.
Impulsive Music, 1993/EMI-April Music, 1993.
Introduced by Billy Joel on *River of Dreams* (Columbia, 93).

**Mr. Jones**
Words and music by Adam Duritz, music by David Bryson.
EMI-Blackwood Music Inc., 1993/Jones Fall Music, 1993.
Best-selling record by Counting Crows from *August and Everything After* (DGC, 93).

**Mister Please**
Words and music by Ted Nugent, Jack Blades, and Tommy Shaw.
Ranch Rock Music, 1992/Warner-Tamerlane Music, 1992/Tranquility Base Songs, 1992/WB Music, 1992.
Best-selling record by Damn Yankees from *Don't Tread on Me* (Warner Bros., 92).

**Mr. Vain** (East German)
English words and music by Steven Levis, Josie Katzmann, and Jay Supreme.
Edition, 1993/WB Music, 1993/Neve Welt Musikverlag (Germany), 1993.
Best-selling record by Culture Beat from *Serenity* (550 Music/Epic, 93).

**Mr. Wendal**
Words and music by Arrested Development.
EMI-Blackwood Music Inc., 1992/Arrested Development Music, 1993.
Best-selling record by Arrested Development from *3 Years 5 Months & 2 Days in the Life of...* (Chrysalis, 92).

**Money in the Bank**
Words and music by John Jarrard, Bob DiPiero, and Mark Sanders.

Alabama Band Music Co., 1993/Wildcountry, 1993/Little Big Town
Music, 1993/American Made Music, 1993/MCA Music, 1993.
Best-selling record by John Anderson from *Solid Ground* (BNA, 93).

**Moon River**
Music by Henry Mancini, words by Johnny Mercer.
Famous Music Corp., 1961.
Introduced by Audrey Hepburn in the film *Breakfast at Tiffany's*
released on *Music from the Films of Audrey Hepburn* (Big Screen/
Giant, 93).

**More and More** (East German)
English words and music by Giora Schein, Oliver Reinecke, Juergen
Katzmann, and Tony Dawson-Harrison.
ICM, 1993/Edition, 1993/Get Into Magic, 1993/WB Music, 1993.
Best-selling record by Captain Hollywood Project from *Love Is Not Sex*
(Imageo, 93).

**Mountain of Tears**
Words and music by Peter Richan.
Peter's Cathedral, 1993.
Introduced by Peter's Cathedral (7 Records, 93).

**My Baby Loves Me**
Words and music by Gretchen Peters.
Sony Cross Keys Publishing Co. Inc., 1993.
Best-selling record by Martina McBride from *That's the Way I Am*
(RCA, 93).

**My Back Pages**
Words and music by Bob Dylan.
Special Rider Music, 1966.
Revived by Bob Dylan on *The 30th Anniversary Concert Celebration*
(Columbia, 93). His all-star backup group includes George Harrison,
Tom Petty, Roger McQuinn,Neil Young, and Eric Clapton.

**My Second Home**
Words and music by Tracy Lawrence, Kenny Beard, and Paul Nelson.
Mike Dunn, 1993/Golden Reed Music, 1993/Sony Tree, 1993.
Best-selling record by Tracy Lawrence from *Alibis* (Atlantic, 93).

**My Sister**
Words and music by Juliana Hatfield.
Juliana Hatfield, 1993.
Best-selling record by The Juliana Hatfield Three from *Become What
You Are* (Mammoth/Atlantic, 93).

# N

**Natural**
Words and music by Arrested Development.
EMI-Blackwood Music Inc., 1993/Arrested Development Music, 1993.
Introduced by Arrested Development on *Unplugged* (Chrysalis, 93).

**Never a Time** (English)
Words and music by Anthony Banks, Phil Collins, and Mike Rutherford.
Anthony Banks, England, 1991/Phil Collins, 1991/Michael Rutherford
    Music, 1991.
Best-selling record by Genesis from *We Can't Dance* (Atlantic, 91).

**Never Keeping Secrets**
Words and music by Babyface (pseudonym for Kenny Edmunds).
Sony Songs, 1993/Ecaf, 1993.
Best-selling record by Babyface from *For the Cool in You* (Epic, 93).

**Never Should've Let You Go**
Words and music by Eric Foster White.
Zomba Music, 1993/4MW, 1993.
Best-selling record by Hi-Five from *Faithful* (Jive, 93).

**New Madrid**
Words and music by Jay Farrar and Jeff Tweedy.
VER Music, 1993/Freedom Songs, 1993/Warner-Tamerlane Music,
    1993.
Best-selling record by Uncle Tupelo in *Anodyne* (Sire, 93).

**Nickel Bags (of Funk)**
Words and music by Digable Planets.
Wide Grooves, 1993/Giro Productions, 1993.
Introduced by Digable Planets on *Reachin' (A New Refutation of Time
    and Space)* (Pendulum/Elektra, 93).

**Night Owl Cafe**
Words and music by John Sebastian.

John Sebastian Music, 1993.
Introduced by John Sebastian on *Tar Beach* (Shanachie, 93).

**No Future in the Past**
Words and music by Vince Gill and Carl Jackson.
Benefit Music, 1992/Famous Music Corp., 1992/Too Strong, 1992.
Best-selling record by Vince Gill from *I Still Believe in You* (MCA, 92).

**No Man's Land**
Words and music by Billy Joel.
Impulsive Music, 1993/EMI-April Music, 1993.
Introduced by Billy Joel on *River of Dreams* (Columbia, 93).

**No Mistakes**
Words and music by Patty Smyth and Kevin Savigar.
EMI-Blackwood Music Inc., 1992/Pink Smoke Music, 1992/Almo
    Music Corp., 1992/Kevin Savigar, 1992.
Best-selling record by Patty Smyth from *Patty Smyth* (MCA, 92).

**No Ordinary Love** (English)
Words and music by Sade Adu and Stuart Matthewman.
Silver Angel Music, 1992/Sony Tunes, 1992/Playhard Music, 1992.
Best-selling record by Sade from *Love Deluxe* (Epic, 92).

**No Rain**
Words and music by Blind Melon.
Heavy Melon, 1993.
Best-selling record by Blind Melon from *Blind Melon* (Capitol, 93).

**No Time to Kill**
Words and music by Clint Black and Hayden Nicholas.
Blackened, 1993.
Best-selling record by Clint Black from *No Time to Kill* (RCA, 93).

**Nobody**
Words and music by David Baerwald.
Almo Music Corp., 1993/Zen of Iniquity, 1993.
Introduced by David Baerwald on *Triage* (A&M, 93).

**Nobody Wins**
Words and music by Radney Foster and Kim Richey.
Polygram Music Publishing Inc., 1992/Julien, 1992/Mighty Nice Music,
    1992.
Best-selling record by Radney Foster from *Del Rio, TX 1959* (Arista,
    92).

**Not Sleeping Around**
Words and music by Ned's Atomic Dustbin.
Polygram International, 1992.

Best-selling record by Ned's Atomic Dustbin from *Are You Normal* (Chaos, 92).

**Nothin' My Love Can't Fix**
Words and music by Joey Lawrence, Alexandra Forbes, and Eric Beall.
Platinum Plateau, 1993/Irving Music Inc., 1993/La Familia, 1993.
Best-selling record by Joey Lawrence from *Joey Lawrence* (Impact/ MCA, 93).

**Numb** (Irish)
Words and music by Edge.
Polygram International, 1993.
Best-selling record by U2 from *Zooropa* (Island, 93).

**Nuthin' But a 'G' Thang**
Words and music by Snoop (pseudonym for Calvin Broadus).
Ain't Nothin' Goin on But Fu-kin, 1992.
Best-selling record by Dr. Dre from *The Chronic* (Death Row/ Interscope/Priority, 92). Leading entry in 'gangsta' rap phenomenon.

# O

**Off the Ground** (English)
Words and music by Paul McCartney.
MPL Communications Inc., 1993.
Introduced by Paul McCartney on *Off the Ground* (Capitol, 93).

**Once upon a Lifetime**
Words and music by Gary Baker and Frank J. Myers.
Zomba Music, 1992/Dixie Stars Music, 1992.
Best-selling record by Alabama from *American Pride* (RCA, 92).

**The One I Love** (Scottish)
Words and music by Stuart Adamson and Bruce Watson.
EMI-10, 1993.
Introduced by Big Country on *The Buffalo Skinners* (Fox/BMG, 93).

**One Last Cry**
Words and music by Brian McKnight, Brandon Barnes, and Melanie
  Barnes.
PRI Music, 1993/Let's Have Lunch Music, 1993/Rejoice, 1993.
Best-selling record by Brian McKnight from *Brian McKnight* (Mercury,
  93).

**One More Last Chance**
Words and music by Vince Gill and Gary Nicholson.
Benefit Music, 1992/Sony Cross Keys Publishing Co. Inc., 1992.
Best-selling record by Vince Gill from *I Still Believe in You* (MCA, 92).

**One Woman**
Words and music by Vassal Benford and Ron Spearman.
Gradington Music, 1992/MCA Music, 1992/Ronnie Onyx, 1992.
Best-selling record by Jade from *Jade to the Max* (Giant/Reprise, 93).

**Only a Woman's Heart** (Irish)
Words and music by Eleanor McEvoy.
EMI-Blackwood Music Inc., 1992/Blue Dandelion, 1992/Little Roz,

1992.
Introduced by Eleanor McEvoy on *Eleanor McEvoy* (Geffen, 93).

**Only Love**
Words and music by Marcus Hummon and Roger Murrah.
Careers-BMG, 1993/Murrah, 1993/Tom Collins Music Corp., 1993.
Best-selling record by Wynonna from *Tell Me Why* (Curb/MCA, 93).

**Ooh Child**
Words and music by Stan Vincent.
EMI Unart Catalogue, 1970/Sleeping Son Music Inc., 1970.
Revived by Dino on *The Way I Am* (EastWest America, 93).

**Ordinary World** (English)
Words and music by Duran Duran.
Copyright Control, 1992.
Best-selling record by Duran Duran from *Duran Duran* (Capitol, 93).

**Our Town**
Words and music by Iris DeMent.
Forerunner Music, 1993/Songs of Iris, 1993.
Introduced by Iris DeMent on *Infamous Angel* (Warner Bros., 93).

**Outbreak of Love** (Australian)
Words and music by Hirst.
Sprint, 1993/Warner-Chappell Music, 1993/Warner-Tamerlane Music,
    1993.
Introduced by Midnight Oil on *Earth & Sun & Moon* (Columbia, 93).

# P

**Paint the White House Black**
Words and music by George Clinton, William Bryant, III, Kerry Gordy, Barrett Strong, and Norman Whitfield.
Stone Agate Music, 1993/Warner-Tamerlane Music, 1993/Exaskeletal, 1993/Aujord Hui, 1993/Yreek, 1993.
Best-selling record by George Clinton from *Hey Man...Smell My Finger* (Paisley Park/Warner Bros., 93).

**Paper Walls**
Words and music by Marc Cohn.
Museum Steps Music, 1992.
Introduced by Marc Cohn on *The Rainy Season* (Atlantic, 93).

**Passionate Kisses**
Words and music by Lucinda Williams.
Lucy Jones Music, 1988/Nomad-Noman, 1988/Warner-Tamerlane Music, 1988.
Revived by Mary-Chapin Carpenter in *Come on, Come on* (Columbia, 92). Introduced by Lucinda Williams on *Lucinda Williams* (Rough/Trade). Won a Grammy Award,      Country Song of the Year, 1993.

**Peace in Our Time** (English)
Words and music by Elvis Costello (pseudonym for DeClan McManus).
Plangent Visions Music, Inc., London, England, 1984.
Revived by Carter USM on *Peace Together* (Island, 93).

**Peace Pipe**
Words and music by Kelly Holland and Audley Freed.
In Stereo, 1993/Acetylene, 1993.
Best-selling record by Cry of Love from *Brother* (Columbia, 93).

**Perfectly Good Guitar**
Words and music by John Hiatt.
Lillybilly, 1993/Bug Music, 1993.
Introduced by John Hiatt on *Perfectly Good Guitar* (A&M, 93).

**Pets**
Words and music by Porno for Pyros.
I'll Hit You Back, 1992/EMI-Virgin, 1992.
Best-selling record by Porno for Pyros from *Porno for Pyros* (Warner Bros., 93).

**Philadelphia**
Words and music by Neil Young.
Silver Fiddle, 1993.
Introduced by Neil Young in the film and soundtrack LP *Philadelphia* (Epic Soundtrax, 93). Nominated for an Academy Award, Song of the Year, 1993.

**Pink Cashmere**
Words and music by Prince.
Controversy Music, 1993/WB Music, 1993.
Introduced by Prince on *The Hits/The B Sides* (Paisley Park/WB, 93).

**Please Forgive Me** (Canadian-English)
Words and music by Bryan Adams and Robert John Lange.
Worksongs, 1993/Zomba Music, 1993.
Best-selling record by Bryan Adams on *So Far So Good* (A&M, 93).

**Plush**
Words and music by Robert DeLeo and Weiland DeLeo.
Floated Music, 1992/EMI-Virgin, 1992.
Best-selling record by Stone Temple Pilots from *Core* (Atlantic, 93).

**Poetry** (Netherlands)
Music by Ad van Dijk, Dutch words by Koen van Dijk, English words by Peter Reeves and Sheldon Harnick.
Introduced by Bill van Dijk and Anne Renolfsson in *Cyrano* (93).

**Posse Love**
Words and music by Anthony Smith and M. Walk.
Polygram International, 1993/Loc'ed Out, 1993.
Introduced by Tone Loc in the film and soundtrack album *Posse* (A&M, 93).

**The Power of Love** (East German)
English words and music by Gunther Mende, Candy DeRouge, Jennifer Rush, and Mary Applegate.
EMI Songs Ltd., 1986/EMI-April Music, 1986.
Revived by Celine Dion on *The Colour of My Love* (550 Music/Epic, 93).

**Precious Time**
Words and music by Darden Smith.

Crooked Fingers, 1993/AGF Music Ltd., 1993.
Introduced by Darden Smith on *Little Victories* (Chaos/Columbia, 93).

**Pride and Joy** (English)
Words and music by David Coverdale and Jimmy Page.
Silver State, 1993/WB Music, 1993/Succubus Music, 1993.
Best-selling record by Coverdale/Page from *Coverdale/Page* (Geffen, 93).

**Prisoner of Life**
Words by Doc Pomus, music by Mack Rebennack.
Stazybo Music, 1986/Skull Music, 1986.
Revived by Annie Ross in the film and soundtrack album *Short Cuts* (Imago, 93). Introduced by Johnny Adams on *Johnny Adams Sings Doc Pomus* (Rounder, 91).

**Prop Me up Beside the Jukebox (If I Die)**
Words and music by Rick Blaylock, Kerry Phillips, and Howard Perdew.
Songwriters Ink, 1992/Texas Wedge, 1992.
Best-selling record by Joe Diffie from *Honky Tonk Attitude* (Epic, 92).

**Pundits and Poets**
Words and music by Patty Larkin.
Lost Lake Arts Music, 1993/Lamartine, 1993.
Introduced by Patty Larkin on *Angels Running* (High Street, 93).

**Punks Jump up to Get Beat Down**
Words and music by Lorenzo Dechalus, Derek Murphy, Ronald Isley, Rudolph Isley, and O'Kelly Lisley.
Rush Town Music Assoc. Labels, 1993/EMI-April Music, 1993/Bovina Music, Inc., 1993.
Introduced by Brand Nubian on *In God We Trust* (Elektra, 93).

**Push th' Little Daisies**
Words and music by Aaron Freeman and Michael Melchiardo.
Warner-Tamerlane Music, 1992/VER Music, 1992/Brown Dog, 1992.
Introduced by Ween on *Pure Guava* (Elektra, 93).

# Q

**Quality Time**
Words and music by Robert Kelly.
Willesden Music, Inc., 1992/R. Kelly Music, 1992.
Best-selling record by Hi-Five from *Keep It Goin' On* (Sire, 92).

**Queen of Memphis**
Words and music by Dave Gibson and Kathy Louvin.
Nocturnal Eclipse Music, 1992/Tillis Tunes, 1992/Varon County, 1992.
Best-selling record by Confederate Railroad from *Confederate Railroad*
    (Atlantic, 92).

# R

**Rain**
Words and music by Madonna Ciccone and Shep Pettibone.
WB Music, 1992/Webo Girl, 1992/Shepsongs, 1992/MCA Music, 1992.
Introduced by Madonna on *Erotica* (Maverick/Sire, 92).

**The Rainy Season**
Words and music by Marc Cohn.
Museum Steps Music, 1992.
Introduced by Marc Cohn on *The Rainy Season* (Atlantic, 93).

**Real World**
Words and music by Geoff Tate, Michael Kamen, Chris DeGarmo,
  Eddie Jackson, Michael Wilton, and Scott Rockenfield.
Tri Ryche, 1992/Sony Songs, 1992/K-Man, 1992/Colpix, 1992.
Introduced by Queensryche in the film and soundtrack of *The Last
  Action Hero* (Columbia, 93).

**Reason to Believe**
Words and music by Tim Hardin.
Alley Music, 1966/Trio Music Co., Inc., 1966.
Revived by Rod Stewart on *Unplugged and Seated* (Warner Bros., 93).

**Rebirth of Slick (Cool Like Dat)**
Words and music by Digable Planets.
Wide Grooves, 1993/Giro Productions, 1993.
Best-selling record by Digable Planets from *Reachin' (A New Refutation
  of Time and Space)* (Pendulum/Elektra, 93).

**Reckless**
Words and music by Jeff Stevens and Michael Clark.
WB Music, 1993/Jeff Stevens, 1993/Warner-Tamerlane Music, 1993/
  Flying Dutchman, 1993.
Best-selling record by Alabama from *Cheap Seats* (RCA, 93).

**The Red Shoes** (English)
Words and music by Kate Bush.

Kate Bush Music, Ltd., London, England, 1993.
Introduced by Kate Bush on *The Red Shoes* (Columbia, 93).

**Regret** (English)
Words and music by Gillian Gilbert, Peter Hook, Stephen Morris,
  Bernard Sumner, and Stephen Hague.
Vitalturn, 1993/WB Music, 1993.
Best-selling record by New Order from *Republic* (Qwest/Warner Bros.,
  93).

**Right Here (Human Nature)/Downtown**
Words and music by Brian Alexander Morgan, John Bettis, Steve
  Porcaro, Tamara Johnson, Genard Parker, Kenny Ortiz, and Gina
  Gomez.
Warner-Tamerlane Music, 1993/Interscope Pearl, 1993/Bam Jams, 1993/
  ATV Music Corp., 1993/John Bettis Music, 1993/WB Music, 1993/
  Playful Music, 1993/G.G. Loves Music, 1993.
Best-selling record by SWV from *It's About Time* (RCA, 93).

**The Right Kind of Love**
Words and music by Tommy Faragher, Lotte Golden, and Robbie Nevil.
MCA Music, 1992/Matak Music, 1992/Madfly Music, 1992/Dresden
  China Music, 1992/WB Music, 1992.
Best-selling record by Jeremy Jordan from *Beverly Hills 90210* TV
  show and soundtrack (Grant/Warner Bros., 92).

**River of Dreams**
Words and music by Billy Joel.
Impulsive Music, 1993/EMI-April Music, 1993.
Best-selling record by Billy Joel on *River of Dreams* (Columbia, 93).
  Nominated for Grammy Awards, Record Song of the Year, 1993, and
  Song of the Year, 1993.

**The Road**
Words and music by Danny O'Keefe.
Warner-Tamerlane Music, 1971.
Revived by Bill Morrissey & Greg Brown on *Friend of Mine* (Philo,
  93).

**Romeo**
Words and music by Dolly Parton.
Velvet Apple Music, 1993.
Best-selling record by Dolly Parton and Friends from *Slow Dancing
  with the Moon* (Columbia, 93). Friends include Tanya Tucker, Mary-
  Chapin Carpenter, Kathy Mattea, Pam Tilly, and Billy Ray Cyrus.

**Rubberband Girl** (English)
Words and music by Kate Bush.

Kate Bush Music, Ltd., London, England, 1993.
Introduced by Kate Bush on *The Red Shoes* (Columbia, 93).

**Ruffneck**
Words and music by MC Lyte, Aquil Davidson, Markel Riley, and
  Walter Scott.
Brooklyn Based, 1993/Top Billin, 1993/Smokin' Sounds, 1993/EMI-
  April Music, 1993/Abdur Rahman, 1993/MCA Music, 1993/Soul
  Assassins Music, 1993/Quick Time, 1993.
Best-selling record by MC Lyte from *Ain't No Other* (First Priority, 93).

**Run to You**
Words and music by Allan Rich and Judd Friedman.
Music of the World, 1992/Nelana Music, 1992/PSO Ltd., 1992/Music by
  Candlelight, 1992.
Best-selling record by Whitney Houston from the film and soundtrack
  album of *The Bodyguard* (Arista, 92). Nominated for a Grammy
  Award, Movie or TV Song of the Year, 1993.

**Runaway Train**
Words and music by Dave Pirner.
WB Music, 1992/LFR Music, 1992.
Best-selling record by Soul Asylum from *Grave Dancers Union*
  (Columbia, 92). Won a Grammy Award,     Rock Song of the Year,
  1993.

**Runaway Wind**
Words and music by Paul Westerberg.
Elegant Mule, 1993.
Introduced by Paul Westerberg on *14 Songs* (Sire/Reprise, 93).

# S

**Said I Loved You...But I Lied** (American-English)
Words and music by Michael Bolton and Robert John Lange.
Warner-Chappell Music, 1993/Mr. Bolton's Music, 1993/Warner-
    Tamerlane Music, 1993/Zomba Music, 1993.
Best-selling record by Michael Bolton from *The One Thing* (Columbia,
    93).

**Sail Across the Water** (Canadian)
Words and music by Jane Siberry.
Wing It, 1993/Bug Music, 1993.
Introduced by Jane Siberry on *When I Was a Boy* (Reprise, 93).

**Saturday Nite** (Scottish)
Words and music by Bill Martin (pseudonym for William MacPherson)
    and Phil Coulter.
Colgems-EMI Music, 1975.
Revived by Ned's Atomic Dustbin in the film and soundtrack album *So
    I Married an Axe Murderer* (Chaos/Columbia, 93).

**Say Anything** (English)
Words and music by Aimee Mann and Jon Brion.
You Can't Take It With You, 1993/Lilyac, 1993.
Introduced by Aimee Mann on *Whatever* (Imago, 93).

**Secret O' Life**
Words and music by James Taylor.
Country Road Music Inc., 1977.
Revived by James Taylor on *Live* (Columbia, 93).

**Send for Me**
Words and music by Sam Dees and Ron Kersey.
Luersrika, 1981/Mercy Kersey, 1981/Irving Music Inc., 1981.
Revived by Gerald Alston on *Always in the Mood* (Motown, 92).

**7**
Words and music by Prince, Jimmie McCracklin, and Lowell Fulson.

Controversy Music, 1992/WB Music, 1992/Warner-Chappell Music, 1992/Budget Music, 1992/Bug Music, 1992.
Best-selling record by Prince and the New Power Generation from the 'symbol' album (Paisley Park/WB, 92).

### Seventh Avenue
Words and music by Rosanne Cash and John Leventhal.
Chelcait Music, 1993/Bug Music, 1993/Lev-a-Tunes, 1993.
Introduced by Rosanne Cash on *The Wheel* (Columbia, 93).

### Sex Me (Parts I & II)
Words and music by Robert Kelly.
Zomba Music, 1993/R. Kelly Music, 1993.
Best-selling record by R. Kelly from *12 Play* (Jive, 93).

### She Don't Know She's Beautiful
Words and music by Bob McDill and Paul Harrison.
Polygram Music Publishing Inc., 1993/Ranger Bob Music, 1993/ Careers-BMG, 1993.
Best-selling record by Sammy Kershaw from *Haunted Heart* (Mercury, 93).

### She Used to Be Mine
Words and music by Ronnie Dunn.
Sony Tree, 1993/Deerfield Court Music, 1993.
Best-selling record by Brooks & Dunn from *Hard Workin' Man* (Arista, 93).

### Ship in a Bottle
Words and music by Amanda McBroom.
McBroom Music, 1981.
Introduced in the musical *Heartbeats* (93).

### Shock Your Mama
Words and music by Carl Sturken, Evan Rogers, and Debbie Gibson.
Possibilities, 1992/EMI-April Music, 1992/Warner-Tamerlane Music, 1992/Could Be Music, 1992.
Introduced by Debbie Gibson on *Body Mind Soul* (Atlantic, 93).

### Shoop
Words and music by Mark Sparks, Cheryl James, Sandy Denton, Otwane Roberts, and Nate Turner.
Unichappell Music Inc., 1992/Placid Music Corp., 1992/Kakalaka Music, 1992/Next Plateau Entertainment, 1992/S.T.M. Music, 1992.
Best-selling record by Salt-N-Pepa from *Very Necessary* (Next Plateau, 93).

### Should've Been a Cowboy
Words and music by Toby Keith.

Songs of Polygram, 1993/Tokeco, 1993.
Best-selling record by Toby Keith from *Toby Keith* (Mercury, 93).

**Show Me Love**
Words and music by Allen George and Fred McFarlane.
Song-a-Tron, 1992/Champion Music, 1992.
Best-selling record by Robin S. from *Show Me Love* (Big Beat/Atlantic, 93).

**Simple Life** (English)
Words and music by Elton John and Bernie Taupin.
Big Pig Music, 1992/Intersong, USA Inc., 1993.
Best-selling record by Elton John from *The One* (MCA, 92).

**Six Feet Deep**
Words and music by Brad Jordan, Michael Barnett, Lionel Richie, Marvin Gaye, and J. Johnson.
N-The Water Publishing, 1993/Jobete Music Co., Inc., 1993/EMI-Blackwood Music Inc., 1993/Straight Cash, 1993/Brockman Enterprises Inc., 1993.
Best-selling record by Geto Boys from *Till Death Do Us Part* (Rap-a-lot/Priority, 93).

**(I Know I Got) Skillz**
Words and music by Jeff Fortson, Shaquille O'Neal, and Meech Wells.
Word Life, 1993/Chrysalis Music Group, 1993/Big Giant Music, 1993/Warner-Chappell Music, 1993.
Best-selling record by Shaquille O'Neal from *Shaq Diesel* (Jive, 93).

**Slam**
Words and music by F. Scruggs, Chylow Parker, Jason Mizell, T. Taylor, and K. Jones.
Chyskillz, 1993/Harris Onyx, 1993/EMI-April Music, 1993.
Best-selling record by Onyx from *Bacdafucup* (JMJ/Columbia, 93).

**Sleeping Satellite** (English)
Words and music by Tasmin Archer, John Beck, and John Hughes.
EMI-Virgin, 1992.
Best-selling record by Tasmin Archer from *Great Expectations* (SBK, 92).

**So Alone**
Words and music by Gerald Levert, Edwin Nicholas, Joe Little, III, and Edward Banks.
Trycep Publishing Co., 1993/Ramal Music Co., 1993/Willesden Music, Inc., 1993.
Best-selling record by Men at Large from *Men at Large* (EastWest, 93).

**So Much Mine**
Words and music by Jonatha Brooke.
Dog Dream, 1993.
Introduced by The Story on *The Angel in the House* (Elektra, 93).

**Solitary Man**
Words and music by Neil Diamond.
Tallyrand Music, 1966.
Revived by Chris Isaak on *San Francisco Days* (Reprise, 93).

**Some Kind of Wonderful**
Words and music by John Ellison.
Crash, 1967/Dandelion Music Co., 1967.
Revived by Buddy Guy on *Feels Like Rain* (Silvertone, 93).

**Some People's Lives**
Words and music by Janis Ian and Kye Fleming.
MCA Music, 1986/Eaglewood, 1986/Irving Music Inc., 1986/Taosongs
    Music, 1986.
Revived by Janis Ian on *Breaking Silence* (Morgan Creek, 93).

**Somebody to Love** (English)
Words and music by Freddie Mercury.
Queen Music Ltd., 1977/Beechwood Music, 1977.
Revived by George Michael and Queen in *Five Live* (Hollywood/
    Elektra, 93).

**Somebody's Baby**
Words and music by Neil Geraldo and Pat Geraldo.
Spyder Mae, 1993/Big Tooth Music Corp., 1993/Chrysalis Music Group,
    1993.
Introduced by Pat Benatar on *Gravity's Rainbow* (Chrysalis/ERG, 93).

**Something in Your Eyes**
Words and music by Babyface (pseudonym for Kenny Edmunds).
Sony Songs, 1993/Ecaf, 1993.
Best-selling record by Bell Biv Devoe on *Hootie Mack* (MCA, 93).

**Something's Goin' On**
Words and music by John Powe, Demetrius Peete, and John Clay.
Undercurrent, 1993/Maverick, 1993/Nomad-Noman, 1993/Warner-
    Tamerlane Music, 1993/Audible Arts, 1993/WB Music, 1993.
Best-selling record by U.N.V. from *Something's Goin' On* (Maverick/
    Sire, 93).

**Sometimes I Forget**
Words and music by Loudon Wainwright, III.
Snowden Music, 1992.
Introduced by Loudon Wainwright III in *History* (Charisma, 92).

**The Song Remembers When**
Words and music by Hugh Prestwood.
Careers-BMG, 1993/Hugh Prestwood, 1993.
Best-selling record by Trisha Yearwood from *The Song Remembers When* (MCA, 93).

**Soon**
Words and music by Casey Kelly and Bob Regan.
Miss Pammy's, 1993/Wood Newton, 1993/Himownself's Music Co., 1993/AMR, 1993/Sierra Home, 1993.
Best-selling record by Tanya Tucker from *Soon* (Liberty, 93).

**Soon**
Words and music by Barry Manilow, Jack Feldman, and Bruce Sussman.
Careers-BMG, 1992/Appogiatura Music Inc., 1992/Camp Songs Music, 1992.
Introduced by Michael Feinstein on *Forever* (Elektra, 93). Featured in the film *Thumbellina* (93).

**Soul to Squeeze**
Words and music by Anthony Kiedis, John Frusciante, Chad Smith, and Flea (pseudonym for Michael Balzary).
Ensign Music, 1993/Moebetoblame Music, 1993.
Best-selling record by Red Hot Chili Peppers from the film and soundtrack album *The Coneheads* (Sire/Reprise, 93).

**Speed of the Sound of Loneliness**
Words and music by John Prine.
Bruised Oranges, 1986/Big Ears Music Inc., 1986/Bug Music, 1986.
Revived by Nanci Griffith on *Other Voices, Other Rooms* (Elektra, 93).

**Split Personality**
Words and music by Michael Ivey.
Colored Folks Music, 1993/Imago Songs, 1993.
Introduced by Basshead on *Not in Kansas Anymore* (Imago, 93).

**Stand Up (Kick Love into Motion)** (English)
Words and music by Steve Clark, Phil Collen, Joe Elliot, and Robert John Lange.
Bludgeon Riffola Music, 1992/Zomba Music, 1992.
Best-selling record by Def Leppard from *Adrenalize* (Mercury, 92).

**Start Choppin'**
Words and music by Joseph Mascis.
Zomba Music, 1993.
Best-selling record by Dinosaur Jr. from *Where You Been* (Sire/WB, 93).

**Stay in My Corner**
Words and music by Wade Fleming, Barrett Strong, and Bobby Miller.
Conrad Music, 1965.
Featured in the play *Two Trains Running* (93).

**Stay with Me** (English)
Words and music by Ron Wood and Rod Stewart.
WB Music, 1972.
Revived by Ron Wood on *Plugged In & Still Standing* (Continuum, 93).

**Steam** (English)
Words and music by Peter Gabriel.
Real World Music, 1992/Pentagon Lipservices Real World, 1993.
Best-selling record by Peter Gabriel from *Us* (Geffen, 92).

**Step It up and Go,** also known as **Bottle It up and Go**
Words and music by Washboard Sam (pseudonym for Robert Brown).
Leeds Music Pty., Ltd., Sydney, Australia, 1940.
Revived by Bob Dylan on *Good As I Been to You* (Columbia, 92).
    Written by Chicago policeman Robert Brown, otherwise known as
    Washboard Sam. Tune has been performed by Leadbelly, Big Bill
    Broonzy, Josh White, and many others.

**Stick It Out** (Canadian)
Words and music by Geddy Lee, Alex Lifeson, and Neal Peart.
Core Music Publishing, 1993.
Best-selling record by Rush from *Counterparts* (Atlantic, 93).

**Still Is Still Moving to Me**
Words and music by Willie Nelson.
Full Nelson, 1993/Longitude Music, 1993.
Introduced by Willie Nelson in *Across the Borderline* (Columbia, 93).

**Still Searchin'** (English)
Words and music by Ray Davies.
Davray Music, Ltd., London, England, 1993.
Introduced by The Kinks on *Phobia* (Columbia, 93).

**Story of My Life**
Words and music by David Thomas.
Polygram Music Publishing Inc., 1993.
Introduced by Pere Ubu on *Story of My Life* (Imago, 93).

**Streets of Philadelphia**
Words and music by Bruce Springsteen.
Bruce Springsteen Publishing, 1993.
Introduced by Bruce Springsteen in the film and soundtrack LP
    *Philadelphia* (Epic Soundtrax, 93). Song      won a Golden Globe

Award for best song for a film, 1993. Won an Academy Award, Best song of the year, 1993.

**Sublime**
Words and music by David Shelzel.
EMI-Blackwood Music Inc., 1993/Wasermusik, 1993.
Best-selling record by The Ocean Blue on *Beneath the Rhythm and Sound* (Sire/Reprise, 93).

**Summer of Drugs**
Words and music by Victoria Williams.
Mumblety Peg, 1990/Careers-BMG, 1990.
Revived by Soul Asylum on *Sweet Relief: A Benefit for Victoria Williams* (Thirsty Ear/Chaos/Columbia, 93).

**Sunday Morning**
Words and music by Maurice White, Sheldon Reynolds, and Allee Willis.
Maurice White, 1993/Sony Music, 1993/Reyshell, 1993/Warner-Tamerlane Music, 1993/Streamline Moderne, 1993.
Best-selling record by Earth, Wind & Fire from *Millennium* (Reprise, 93).

**Supermodel**
Words and music by Juliana Hatfield.
Juliana Hatfield, 1993.
Introduced by The Juliana Hatfield Three on *Become What You Are* (Mammoth/Atlantic, 93).

**Sure Love**
Words and music by Hal Ketchum and Gary Burr.
Foreshadow Songs, Inc., 1992/Songs of Polygram, 1993/MCA Music, 1993/Gary Burr Music, 1993.
Best-selling record by Hal Ketchum from *Sure Love* (Curb, 92).

**Sweat (A la la la la Long)**
Words and music by Ian Lewis.
Rock Pop Music, 1993.
Best-selling record by Inner Circle from *Bad Boys* (Big Beat/Atlantic, 93).

**Sweet Evening Breeze**
Words and music by John Mellencamp.
Full Keel, 1993.
Introduced by John Mellencamp on *Human Wheels* (Mercury, 93).

**Sweet Thing** (English)
Words and music by Mick Jagger.

Promopub B. V., CH-1017 Amsterdam, Netherlands, 1992.
Introduced by Mick Jagger on *Wandering Spirit* (Atlantic, 93).

**Sweet Thing**
Words and music by Chaka Khan and Tony Maiden.
MCA Music, 1975.
Revived by Mary J. Blige from *What's the 411?* (Uptown/MCA, 92).

# T

**Take a Look**
Words and music by Clyde Otis.
Iza, 1967.
Revived by Natalie Cole on *Take a Look* (Elektra, 93).

**Tarbelly and Featherfoot**
Words and music by Victoria Williams.
Mumblety Peg, 1990/Careers-BMG, 1990.
Revived by Lou Reed on *Sweet Relief: A Benefit for Victoria Williams*
    (Thirsty Ear/Chaos/Columbia, 93).

**Teahouse on the Tracks**
Words and music by Donald Fagen.
Freejunket Music, 1993.
Introduced by Donald Fagen on *Kamakiriad* (Reprise, 93).

**Tell Me It's Not True** (English)
Words and music by Willie Russell.
Introduced in America by Stephanie Lawrence in *Blood Brothers* (93).

**Tell Me Why**
Words and music by Karla Bonoff.
Seagrape Music Inc., 1988.
Revived by Wynonna on *Tell Me Why* (Curb, 93).

**Tender Moment**
Words and music by Lee Roy Parnell, Rory Bourke, and Lewis Moore.
Polygram International, 1993/R-Bar-P, 1993/De Burgo, 1993/New
    Songs, 1993/Mama Guitar, 1993.
Best-selling record by Lee Roy Parnell from *On the Road* (Arista, 93).

**Thank God for You**
Words and music by Mark Miller and Mac McAnally.
Traveling Zoo, 1993/Beginner Music, 1993.
Best-selling record by Sawyer Brown from *Outskirts of Town* (Curb,
    93).

**That Summer**
Words and music by Pat Alger, Sandy Mahl, and Garth Brooks.
Bait and Beer, 1992/Forerunner Music, 1992/Major Bob Music, 1992/No Fences Music, 1992.
Best-selling record by Garth Brooks from *The Chase* (Liberty, 92).

**That's the Way Love Goes**
Words and music by Janet Jackson, James Harris, III, and Terry Lewis.
Black Ice Music, 1992/Flyte Tyme Tunes, 1992.
Best-selling record by Janet Jackson from *janet* (Virgin, 93). Introduced in the film and soundtrack of *Mo Money* (92). Won a Grammy Award,　　Best R&B Song of the Year, 1993.

**That's What I Think**
Words and music by Cyndi Lauper, Rob Hyman, Allee Willis, and Eric Bazilian.
Rella Music Corp., 1993/Warner-Tamerlane Music, 1993/Streamline Moderne, 1993/Dub Notes, 1993/Human Boy Music, 1993.
Introduced by Cyndi Lauper on *Hat Full of Stars* (Epic, 93).

**That's What Love Can Do** (English)
Words and music by Mike Stock, Matt Aitken, and Pete Waterman.
All Boys USA Music, 1993.
Best-selling record by Boy Krazy from *Boy Krazy* (Next Plateau/London, 93).

**There She Goes** (English)
Words and music by L. A. Mavers.
Go! Discs Ltd., England, 1989.
Revived by The Boo Radleys in the film and soundtrack album *So I Married an Axe Murderer* (Chaos/Columbia, 93). Original version by the LA's.

**These Days**
Words and music by Jackson Browne.
Open Window Music Co., 1973.
Revived by The Golden Palominos in *This Is How It Feels* (Restless, 93).

**This Is a Test** (English)
Words and music by Elvis Costello (pseudonym for DeClan McManus).
Plangent Visions Music, Inc., London, England, 1993.
Introduced by Wendy James on *Now Ain't the Time for Your Tears* (DGC, 93).

**A Thousand Miles from Nowhere**
Words and music by Dwight Yoakam.
Coal Dust West, 1993/Warner-Tamerlane Music, 1993.
Best-selling record by Dwight Yoakam from *This Time* (Reprise, 93).

**Three Flights Up**
Words and music by Frank Christian.
Frank Christian Music, 1990.
Revived by Nanci Griffith in *Other Voices, Other Rooms* (Elektra, 93).

**Three Little Pigs**
Words and music by William Manspeaker and Marc Levinthal.
Jello-R-Us, 1993/Schmemetone, 1993/Chrysalis Music Group, 1993.
Best-selling record by Green Jelly from the video *Cereal Killer Soundtrack* (Zoo, 93). Song was eventually released as a single.

**Through Your Hands**
Words and music by John Hiatt.
Lillybilly, 1989/Bug Music, 1989.
Revived by David Crosby on *A Thousand Roads* (Atlantic, 93).

**Time and Chance**
Words and music by Mark Jordan and Mark Denard, words and music by Color Me Badd.
Brittlesse, 1993/Me Good Music, 1993.
Best-selling record by Color Me Badd from *Time and Chance* (Giant, 93).

**Time Passes**
Music by Randy Courts, words by Mark St. Germain.
Introduced by Daniel Jenkins in *Johnny Pye and the Fool Killer* (93).

**Too Busy Being in Love**
Words and music by Victoria Shaw and Gary Burr.
Gary Morris Music, 1992/MCA Music, 1992/Gary Burr Music, 1992.
Best-selling record by Doug Stone from *From the Heart* (Epic, 92).

**Too Many Angels**
Words and music by Jackson Browne.
Swallow Turn Music, 1993.
Introduced by Jackson Browne on *I'm Alive* (Elektra, 93).

**Too Many Ways to Fall**
Words and music by Charlie Sexton, Tonio K. (pseudonym for Steve Krikorian), Chris Layton, and Tommy Shannon.
Sextunes Music, 1992/MCA Music, 1992/WB Music, 1992/
Pressmancherry, 1992/CMI America, 1992.
Best-selling record by Arc Angels from *Arc Angels* (DGC/Geffen, 92).

**Too Young to Die**
Words and music by Jimmy Webb.
White Oak Songs, 1993.
Introduced by David Crosby on *A Thousand Roads* (Atlantic, 93). Also recorded by Jimmy Webb on *Suspending Disbelief* (Elektra, 93).

**True Love**
Words and music by Cole Porter.
Chappell & Co., Inc., 1956.
Revived by Elton John & Kiki Dee on *Duets* (MCA, 93).

**29 Palms** (English)
Words and music by Robert Plant, Chris Blackwell, Charlie Jones, Doug
    Boyle, and Phil Johnstone.
EMI-Virgin, 1993.
Introduced by Robert Plant on *Fate of Nations* (Es Paranza, 93).

**Two Princes**
Words and music by Spin Doctors.
Sony Songs, 1992/Mow B' Jow Music, 1992.
Best-selling record by The Spin Doctors from *Pocket Full of Kryptonite*
    (Epic Associated, 92).

**Two Thousand Years**
Words and music by Billy Joel.
Impulsive Music, 1993/EMI-April Music, 1993.
Introduced by Billy Joel on *River of Dreams* (Columbia, 93).

# U

**The Ugly Truth**
Words and music by Matthew Sweet.
EMI-Blackwood Music Inc., 1992/Charm Trap Music, 1992.
Best-selling record by Matthew Sweet from *Altered Beast* (Zoo, 93).

**Unconditional Love**
Words and music by Luther Campbell.
Zomba Music, 1993/Art & Rhythm, 1993.
Introduced by Hi-Five in the film and soundtrack album *Menace II Society* (Jive, 93).

**U.N.I.T.Y.**
Words and music by Doris Owens and Joe Sample.
Queen Latifah, 1993/Four Knights Music Co., 1993/Music of the World, 1993.
Best-selling record by Queen Latifah from *Black Reign* (Motown, 93).

# V

**Very Special**
Words and music by William Jeffery and Lisa Peters.
WB Music, 1993/Great Walrus Ltd., 1993/Jeffix Music Co., 1993.
Best-selling record by Big Daddy Kane featuring Spinderella, L.
    Williams and K. Anderson from *Looks Like a Job For...* (Cold
    Chillin/Warner Bros., 93).

# W

**Walk on the Ocean**
Words and music by Dean Dinning, Randy Guss, Todd Nichols, and
Glen Phillips.
Sony Music, 1992/Wet Sprocket Songs, 1992.
Best-selling record by Toad the Wet Sprocket from *Fear* (Columbia,
92).

**Walk Through the World**
Words and music by Marc Cohn and John Leventhal.
Museum Steps Music, 1993/Lev-a-Tunes, 1993.
Introduced by Marc Cohn on *The Rainy Season* (Atlantic, 93).

**Walkaway Joe**
Words and music by Vince Melamed and Greg Barnhill.
Warner-Tamerlane Music, 1992/Warner-Refuge Music Inc., 1992/Patrick
Joseph, 1992.
Best-selling record by Trisha Yearwood from *Hearts in Armor* (MCA,
92).

**Walking in My Shoes** (English)
Words and music by Martin Gore.
EMI-Blackwood Music Inc., 1993.
Best-selling record by Depeche Mode from *Songs of Faith and Devotion*
(Mute/Reprise, 93).

**The Wanderer Starring Johnny Cash** (Irish)
Words and music by U2.
Polygram International, 1993.
Introduced by Johnny Cash on U2's *Zooropa* (Island, 93)

**Wannagirl**
Words and music by Keith Thomas and Tony Haynes.
Sony Music, 1993/Yellow Elephant Music, 1993/Large Giant, 1993/
Prosthytumes, 1993.

Best-selling record by Jeremy Jordan from *Try My Love* (Giant/Reprise, 93).

**Weak**
Words and music by Brian Alexander Morgan.
Bam Jams, 1993.
Best-selling record by SWV from *It's About Time* (RCA, 93).

**The Wedge**
Words and music by Trey Anastasio and Tom Marshall.
Who Is She Music, 1993.
Introduced by Phish on *Rift* (Elektra, 93).

**We'll Burn That Bridge**
Words and music by Ronnie Dunn and Don Cook.
Sony Tree, 1993.
Best-selling record by Brooks & Dunn from *Hard Workin' Man* (Arista, 93).

**We've Been Had**
Words and music by Jay Farrar and Jeff Tweedy.
VER Music, 1993/Freedom Songs, 1993/Warner-Tamerlane Music, 1993.
Best-selling record by Uncle Tupelo on *Anodyne* (Sire, 93).

**What Do We Care**
Words by Leslee Bricusse, music by Henry Mancini.
RET Music Inc., 1993.
Introduced by Alley Cats in *Tom & Jerry* (93).

**What If I Came Knocking**
Words and music by John Mellencamp.
Full Keel, 1993.
Introduced by John Mellencamp on *Human Wheels* (Mercury, 93).

**What Might Have Been**
Words and music by Porter Howell, Dwayne O'Brien, and Brady Seals.
Square West, 1993/Howlin' Hits Music, 1993.
Best-selling record by Little Texas from *Big Time* (Warner Bros., 93).

**What Part of No**
Words and music by Wayne Perry and Gerald Smith.
Zomba Music, 1992/O-Tex Music, 1992.
Best-selling record by Lorrie Morgan from *Watch Me* (BNA, 92).

**What's My Name**
Words and music by Snoop (pseudonym for Calvin Broadus).
Suge, 1993.

Introduced by Snoop Doggy Dogg on *Doggy Style* (Death Row/ Interscope, 93).

**What's Up**
Words and music by Linda Perry.
Stuck in the Throat, 1993/Famous Music Corp., 1993.
Best-selling record by 4 Non Blondes from *Bigger, Better, Faster, More!* (Interscope, 93).

**What's Up Doc? (Can We Rock)**
Words and music by R. Roachford, J. Jones, L. Maturine, Kevin McKenzie, and Shaquille O'Neal.
Willesden Music, Inc., 1993/CPMK, 1993/Zomba Music, 1993/Scratch 'N' Source, 1993/Chrysalis Music Group, 1993/EMI-April Music, 1993.
Best-selling record by Fu-Schnickens with Shaquille O'Neal from *Shaq Diesel* (Jive, 93).

**The Wheel**
Words and music by Rosanne Cash.
Chelcait Music, 1993/Bug Music, 1993.
Introduced by Rosanne Cash on *The Wheel* (Columbia, 93).

**When I Fall in Love**
Words and music by Edward Heyman and Victor Young.
Chappell & Co., Inc., 1952/Intersong, USA Inc., 1952.
Revived by Celine Dion and Clive Griffin in the film and soundtrack album *Sleepless in Seattle* (Epic Soundtrax, 93).

**When Love Was Young**
Words and music by Iris DeMent.
Forerunner Music, 1992/Songs of Iris, 1992.
Introduced by Iris Dement in *Infamous Angel* (WB, 93).

**When My Ship Comes In**
Words and music by Clint Black and Hayden Nicholas.
Howlin' Hits Music, 1992.
Best-selling record by Clint Black from *The Hard Way* (RCA, 92).

**When Two Times Two Are Five**
Words and music by Jonatha Brooke.
Dog Dream, 1993.
Introduced by The Story in *The Angel in the House* (Elektra, 93).

**Where I'm From**
Words and music by Digable Planets.
Wide Grooves, 1993/Giro Productions, 1993.
Introduced by Digable Planets in *Reachin' (A New Refutation of Time and Space)* (Pendulum/Elektra, 93).

**Who Is It**
Words and music by Michael Jackson.
Mijac Music, 1991/Warner-Tamerlane Music, 1991.
Best-selling record by Michael Jackson from *Dangerous* (Epic, 91).

**Who Let In the Rain**
Words and music by Cyndi Lauper and Allee Willis.
Rella Music Corp., 1993/EMI-Virgin, 1993/Streamline Moderne, 1993.
Introduced by Cyndi Lauper on *Hat Full of Stars* (Epic, 93).

**Who Was in My Room Last Night**
Words and music by Butthole Surfers.
Latino Buggerveil Music, 1993.
Introduced by Butthole Surfers in *Independent Worm Saloon* (Capitol, 93).

**A Whole New World (Aladdin's Theme)** (American-English)
Music by Alan Menken, words by Tim Rice.
Wonderland Music, 1992/Walt Disney Music, 1992.
Best-selling record by Peabo Bryson and Regina Belle from the film and soundtrack *Aladdin* (Walt Disney, 92). Won a 1992 Academy Award as best song. Won Grammy Awards. Nominated for a Grammy Award, Best Record of the Year, 1993.

**Whoomp! (There It Is)**
Words and music by Tag Team.
Alvert Music, 1993.
Best-selling record by Tag Team from *Whoomp! (There It Is)* (Life, 93). The catch-phrase of theyear.

**Whoot, There It Is**
Words and music by Johnny McGowan and Nathaniel Orange.
Jamie Music Publishing Co., 1993/Kole, Moke & Noke, 1993.
Best-selling record by 95 South from *Quad City Knock* (Wrap, 93).

**Why Didn't I Think of That**
Words and music by Bob McDill and Paul Harrison.
Polygram Music Publishing Inc., 1985/Unichappell Music Inc., 1985/Ranger Bob Music, 1985.
Best-selling record by Doug Stone from *From the Heart* (Epic, 92).

**Why Must We Wait Until Tonight** (Canadian-English)
Words and music by Bryan Adams and Robert John Lange.
Almo Music Corp., 1992/Badams Music, 1992/Zomba Music, 1992.
Introduced by Tina Turner in the film and soundtrack album *What's Love Got to Do with It* (Virgin, 93).

**Wichita Lineman**
Words and music by Jimmy Webb.

Canopy Music Inc., 1966.
Revived by Freedy Johnston on *Unlucky* (Bar/None, 93).

**Wild Horses** (English)
Words and music by Mick Jagger and Keith Richards.
ABKCO Music Inc., 1970.
Revived by The Sundays on *Blind* (DGC, 92).

**Wild, Wild Life**
Words and music by David Byrne.
Index Music, 1986.
Revived by Wailing Souls in the film and soundtrack album *Cool Runnings* (Chaos/Columbia, 93).

**Wild World** (English)
Words and music by Cat Stevens.
Sony Tunes, 1970/Salafa Ltd. (England), 1970.
Revived by Mr. Big on *Bump Ahead* (Atlantic, 93).

**Will You Be There**
Words and music by Michael Jackson.
Mijac Music, 1991/Warner-Tamerlane Music, 1991.
Best-selling record by Michael Jackson from the film and soundtrack album *Free Willy* (MJJ/Epic, 93). Introduced on *Dangerous* (Epic, 91).

**Wings**
Music by Jeffrey Lunden, words by Arthur Perlman.
Introduced by Linda Stephens in *Wings* (93).

**A Wink and a Smile**
Words and music by Marc Shaiman and Ramsey McLean.
TSP Music, Inc., 1992/Triple Star Music, 1992/Winding Brook Way Music, 1992/Ram-Page Publishing Ltd., 1992.
Introduced by Harry Connick, Jr. in the film and soundtrack *Sleepless in Seattle* (Epic Soundtrax, 93). Nominated for an Academy Award, Best Song of the Year, 1993.

**With One Look**
Words and music by Andrew Lloyd Webber, Don Black, Christopher Hampton, and Amy Powers.
Music by Candlelight, 1993/PSO Ltd., 1993.
Revived by Barbra Streisand in *The Broadway Album* (Columbia, 93). Written for the musical *Sunset Boulevard*.

**Won't Get Fooled Again** (English)
Words and music by Peter Townshend.
ABKCO Music Inc., 1971/Suolabaf Music, 1971/Towser Tunes Inc., 1971.

Revived by Van Halen on *Van Halen Live: Right Here, Right Now* (Warner Bros., 93).

**Work for Food**
Words and music by Jon Easdale.
Longitude Music, 1993/Binky Music, 1993.
Introduced by Dramarama on *Hi-Fi Sci-Fi* (Chameleon, 93).

**World Class Fad**
Words and music by Paul Westerberg.
Elegant Mule, 1993.
Introduced by Paul Westerberg on *14 Songs* (Sire/Reprise, 93).

**Worlds Apart**
Words and music by Jude Cole and Ron Anielo.
EMI-Blackwood Music Inc., 1992/Coleision Music, 1992/Mike Curb Productions, 1992.
Introduced by Jude Cole on *Start the Car* (Reprise, 92).

# Y

**You and Me Go Way Back**
Words and music by John Sebastian.
John Sebastian Music, 1993.
Introduced by John Sebastian on *Tar Beach* (Shanachie, 93).

**You Can't Sit Down**
Words and music by Dee Clark, Cornell Muldrew, and Kal Mann.
Conrad Music, 1960.
Featured in the play *The Sisters Rosensweig* (93).

**You Won't Let Me In**
Words and music by Rosanne Cash.
Chelcait Music, 1993/Bug Music, 1993.
Introduced by Rosanne Cash on *The Wheel* (Columbia, 93).

**You've Lost That Lovin' Feelin'**
Words and music by Barry Mann, Cynthia Weil, and Phil Spector.
Screen Gems-EMI Music Inc., 1964/Mother Bertha Music, Inc., 1964/
    ABKCO Music Inc., 1964.
Revived by Neil Diamond and Dolly Parton on *Songs from the Brill
    Building* (Columbia, 93).

# Lyricists & Composers Index

# Lyricists & Composers Index

# Lyricists & Composers Index

Clivilles, Rob
  It's Gonna Be a Lovely Day
Cochran, Eddie
  C'mon Everybody
Cohen, Leonard
  Closing Time
Cohn, Marc
  Paper Walls
  The Rainy Season
  Walk Through the World
Cole, David
  It's Gonna Be a Lovely Day
Cole, Jude
  Worlds Apart
Collen, Phil
  Stand Up (Kick Love into Motion)
Collins, Phil
  Both Sides of the Story
  Hero
  Never a Time
Color Me Badd
  Time and Chance
Colvin, Shawn
  I Don't Know Why
Conner, Dino
  Knockin' Da Boots
Cook, Don
  We'll Burn That Bridge
Cordes, Atrel
  Looking Through Patient Eyes
Costello, Elvis
  I Almost Had a Weakness
  The Letter Home
  London's Brilliant
  The Lovers That Never Were
  Peace in Our Time
  This Is a Test
Coulter, Phil
  Saturday Nite
Courts, Randy
  Time Passes
Coverdale, David
  Pride and Joy
Creatore, Luigi
  Can't Help Falling in Love
Creole, D.
  Dazzey Duks

Criss, Anthony
  Hey Mr. DJ
Crosby, David
  Hero
D'arby, Terence Trent
  Delicate
Davidson, Aquil
  Ruffneck
Davies, Ray
  Hatred (A Duet)
  Still Searchin'
Davis, J.
  Award Tour
Davis, Stephanie
  It's All in the Heart
  Learning to Live Again
Dawson-Harrison, Tony
  More and More
Deal, Kim
  Cannonball
Dechalus, Lorenzo
  Punks Jump up to Get Beat Down
Dees, Sam
  Send for Me
DeGarmo, Chris
  Real World
DeLeo, Robert
  Plush
DeLeo, Weiland
  Plush
DeMent, Iris
  Infamous Angel
  Our Town
  When Love Was Young
Denard, Mark
  Time and Chance
Denton, Sandy
  Shoop
DeRouge, Candy
  The Power of Love
Devaney, Ian
  In All the Right Places
Diamond, Neil
  Solitary Man
Difford, Chris
  Everything in the World
Digable Planets
  Nickel Bags (of Funk)

# Lyricists & Composers Index

# Lyricists & Composers Index

# Lyricists & Composers Index

# Lyricists & Composers Index

# Important Performances Index

Songs are listed under the works in which they were introduced or given significant renditions. The index is organized into major sections by performance medium: Album, Movie, Musical, Performer, Revue, Television Show.

## Album

**109**

The One Thing
  Said I Loved You...But I Lied
Only What I Feel
  Blame It on Your Heart
Ooooooohhh...On the TLC Tip
  Hat 2 Da Back
Other Voices, Other Rooms
  Speed of the Sound of Loneliness
  Three Flights Up
Out of Control
  Everything Comes Down to Money
    and Love
Outskirts of Town
  Thank God for You
Pablo Honey
  Creep
Pain Makes You Beautiful
  Being Simple
Painted Desert Serenade
  Jessie
Patty Smyth
  No Mistakes
Peace Together
  Peace in Our Time
Perfectly Good Guitar
  Buffalo River Home
  Perfectly Good Guitar
Perverse
  The Devil You Know
Philadelphia
  Philadelphia
  Streets of Philadelphia
Phobia
  Hatred (A Duet)
  Still Searchin'
Pieces
  Ain't Going Down (Til the Sun Comes
    Up)
  American Honky Tonk Bar Association
Plugged In & Still Standing
  Stay with Me
Pocket Full of Kryptonite
  Two Princes
Porno for Pyros
  Cursed Female
  Pets
Portrait
  Here We Go Again

Posse
  Posse Love
The Predator
  Check Yo Self
  It Was a Good Day
Psycho Derelict
  English Boy
Pure Country
  Heartland
Pure Guava
  Push th' Little Daisies
Q3
  Love U More
Quad City Knock
  Whoot, There It Is
The Rainy Season
  Paper Walls
  The Rainy Season
  Walk Through the World
Reachin' (A New Refutation of Time and
    Space)
  Nickel Bags (of Funk)
  Rebirth of Slick (Cool Like Dat)
  Where I'm From
Red and Rio Grande
  I Don't Call Him Daddy
The Red Shoes
  Eat the Music
  The Red Shoes
  Rubberband Girl
Republic
  Regret
Rid of Me
  50 Ft. Queenie
  Highway 61 Revisited
Rift
  The Wedge
River of Dreams
  All About Soul
  A Minor Variation
  No Man's Land
  River of Dreams
  Two Thousand Years
Roll with the Flava
  Hey Mr. DJ
San Francisco Days
  Beautiful Homes

117

Whatever
  Say Anything
What's Love Got to Do with It
  I Don't Wanna Fight
  Why Must We Wait Until Tonight
What's the 411?
  Sweet Thing
The Wheel
  Seventh Avenue
  The Wheel
  You Won't Let Me In
When I Was a Boy
  Calling All Angels
  Love Is Everything
  Sail Across the Water
Where You Been
  Start Choppin'
Whoomp! (There It Is)
  Whoomp! (There It Is)
Winter Light
  Heartbeats Accelerating
Yes I Am
  I'm the Only One
Zooropa
  Lemon
  Numb
  The Wanderer Starring Johnny Cash

# Movie

The Age of Innocence
  Marble Halls
Aladdin
  Friend Like Me
  A Whole New World (Aladdin's
    Theme)
Annie Warbucks
  Leave It to the Girls
Beethoven's 2nd
  The Day I Fall in Love
Benny and Joon
  I'm Gonna Be (500 Miles)
The Bodyguard
  I Have Nothing
  I Will Always Love You
  I'm Every Woman
  It's Gonna Be a Lovely Day
  Run to You

Boomerang
  Love Shoulda Brought You Home
Breakfast at Tiffany's
  Moon River
Cereal Killer Soundtrack
  Three Little Pigs
The Coneheads
  Soul to Squeeze
Cool Runnings
  I Can See Clearly Now
  Wild, Wild Life
The Crying Game
  The Crying Game
Free Willy
  Will You Be There
Indecent Proposal
  In All the Right Places
The Last Action Hero
  Big Gun
  Real World
The Last of the Mohicans
  I Will Find You
Menace II Society
  Unconditional Love
Meteor Man
  It's for You
Mo' Money
  That's the Way Love Goes
People Get Ready: A Tribute to Curtis
    Mayfield
  Choice of Colours
Philadelphia
  Philadelphia
  Streets of Philadelphia
Poetic Justice
  Again
Posse
  Posse Love
Pure Country
  Heartland
Short Cuts
  Prisoner of Life
Sleepless in Seattle
  When I Fall in Love
  A Wink and a Smile
Sliver
  Can't Help Falling in Love

So I Married an Axe Murderer
  Saturday Nite
  There She Goes
Super Mario Brothers
  Almost Unreal
The Three Musketeers
  All for Love
Thumbellina
  Soon
Tom and Jerry
  Friends to the End
  What Do We Care
What's Love Got to Do with It
  I Don't Wanna Fight
  Why Must We Wait Until Tonight

## Musical

Blood Brothers
  Marilyn Monroe
  Tell Me It's Not True
Cyrano
  Even Then
  Poetry
The Girl Who Was Plugged In
  Eyes That Never Lie
Goodbye Girl
  How Can I Win
Heartbeats
  Ship in a Bottle
Johnny Pye and the Fool Killer
  Time Passes
Kiss of the Spider Woman
  The Day After That
  Dear One
The Red Shoes
  Be Somewhere
Sunset Boulevard
  With One Look
Tommy
  I Believe My Own Eyes
Wings
  Wings

## Performer

AC/DC
  Big Gun

Ace of Base
  All That She Wants
Adams, Bryan
  All for Love
  Please Forgive Me
Adams, Johnny
  Prisoner of Life
Aerosmith
  Amazing
  Cryin'
  Livin' on the Edge
Alabama
  Hometown Honeymoon
  Once upon a Lifetime
  Reckless
Alley Cats
  What Do We Care
Alston, Gerald
  Send for Me
Anderson, John
  Money in the Bank
Arc Angels
  Too Many Ways to Fall
Archer, Tasmin
  Sleeping Satellite
Arrested Development
  Mr. Wendal
  Natural
Ash, Daniel
  Get out of Control
Astley, Rick
  Hopelessly
Babyface
  Never Keeping Secrets
Baerwald, David
  Nobody
Basshead
  Split Personality
Beavis and Butt-Head
  Come to Butt-Head
Beck
  Loser
Bell Biv Devoe
  Gangsta
  Something in Your Eyes
Belle, Regina
  A Whole New World (Aladdin's
    Theme)

# Important Performances Index — Performer

## Play

## Television Show

# Awards Index

A list of songs nominated for Academy Awards by the Academy of Motion Picture Arts and Sciences and Grammy Awards from the National Academy of Recording Arts and Sciences. Asterisks indicate the winners.

## 1993

Academy Award
  Again
  The Day I Fall in Love
  Philadelphia
  Streets of Philadelphia*
  A Wink and a Smile
Grammy Award
  Ain't That Lonely Yet
  Anniversary
  Are You Gonna Go My Way
  Can We Talk
  Chattahoochee
  Cryin'
  Does He Love You
  Friend Like Me
  The Hard Way
  Harvest Moon
  Heaven Knows
I Don't Wanna Fight
I Have Nothing
I Will Always Love You*
I'd Do Anything for Love (But I
  Won't Do That)
If I Ever Lose My Faith In You
Little Miracles (Happen Every Day)
Livin' on the Edge
Passionate Kisses*
River of Dreams
Run to You
Runaway Train*
That's the Way Love Goes*
A Whole New World (Aladdin's
  Theme)*
A Whole New World (Aladdin's
  Theme)
A Whole New World (Aladdin's
  Theme)*

# List of Publishers

A directory of publishers of the songs included in *Popular Music,* 1993. Publishers that are members of the American Society of Composers, Authors, and Publishers or whose catalogs are available under ASCAP license are indicated by the designation (ASCAP). Publishers that have granted performing rights to Broadcast Music, Inc., are designated by the notation (BMI). Publishers whose catalogs are represented by The Society of Composers, Authors and Music Publishers of Canada, are indicated by the designation (SOCAN).

The addresses were gleaned from a variety of sources, including ASCAP, BMI, SOCAN, and *Billboard* magazine. As in any volatile industry, many of the addresses may become outdated quickly. In the interim between the book's completion and its subsequent publication, some publishers may have been consolidated into others or changed hands. This is a fact of life long endured by the music business and its constituents. The data collected here, and throughout the book, are as accurate as such circumstances allow.

**A**

Abdur Rahman (ASCAP)
see MCA Music

ABKCO Music Inc. (BMI)
1700 Broadway
New York, New York 10019

Acetylene (ASCAP)
see In Stereo

Across 110th Street Music (ASCAP)
see EMI Music Publishing

Act Five (BMI)
see Windswept Pacific

Acuff Rose Music (BMI)
65 Music Square West
Nashville, Tennessee 37203

After Berger (ASCAP)
see Warner-Chappell Music

AGF Music Ltd. (ASCAP)
1500 Broadway, Suite 2805
New York, New York 10036

Aggressive (ASCAP)
see EMI Music Publishing

Ain't Nothin' Goin on But Fu-kin (ASCAP)
see Sony Music

Alabama Band Music Co. (ASCAP)
803 18th Avenue S.
Nashville, Tennessee 37203

J. Albert & Sons Music (ASCAP)
c/o Freddy Bienstock Ent.
1619 Broadway, 11th Fl.
New York, New York 10019

Algee Music Corp. (BMI)
see Al Gallico Music Corp.

All About Me Music (BMI)
see MCA Music

All Boys USA Music (BMI)
see Terrace Music

Alley Music (BMI)
1619 Broadway, 11th Fl.
New York, New York 10019

Almo/Irving
1358 N. LaBrea
Los Angeles, California 90028

Almo Music Corp. (BMI)
360 N. La Cienega
Los Angeles, California 90048

Alvert Music (BMI)
see Bellmark Records

American Made Music (BMI)
c/o Little Big Town Music
803 18th Avenue, S.
Nashville, Tennessee 37203

AMR (ASCAP)
54 Music Sq. E.
Nashville, Tennessee 37203

Appogiatura Music Inc. (BMI)
see BMG Music

Arrested Development Music (BMI)
see EMI Music Publishing

Art & Rhythm (ASCAP)
see Zomba Music

ATV Music Corp. (BMI)
6363 Sunset Blvd
Los Angeles, California 90028

Audible Arts (BMI)
see Warner-Chappell Music

Aujord Hui (BMI)
see Warner-Chappell Music

Avant Garde Music (ASCAP)
9229 Sunset Blvd.,
Suite 813
Los Angeles, California 90069

# B

B-Flat Publishing Co. (BMI)
c/o Copyright Service Bureau
221 W. 57th Street
New York, New York 10019

B. Funk (ASCAP)
see Warner-Chappell Music

Badams Music (ASCAP)
see Almo Music Corp.

Bait and Beer (ASCAP)
c/o Terrell Tye
P.O. Box 120657
Nashville, Tennessee 37212

Bam Jams (ASCAP)
see Warner-Chappell Music

Bash (ASCAP)
see Sony Music

Basically Zappo Music (ASCAP)
see Warner-Chappell Music

Beartooth Music (BMI)
see EMI Music Publishing

Beechwood Music (BMI)
see EMI Music Publishing

Beef Puppet (ASCAP)
see MCA Music

Beggar's Banquet
see Warner-Chappell Music

Beginner Music (ASCAP)
P.O. Box 2532
Muscle Shoals, Alabama 35662

Bellmark Records
7060 Hollywood Blvd., 2nd Fl.
Hollywood, California 90028

Benefit Music (BMI)
7250 Beverly Blvd
Los Angeles, California 90036

Best of Breed Music (ASCAP)
Box 5645
Berkeley, California 94705

John Bettis Music (ASCAP)
317 23rd St
Santa Monica, California 90402

Big Ears Music Inc. (ASCAP)
c/o Sy Miller
565 Fifth Avenue, Suite 1001
New York, New York 10017

Big Giant Music (BMI)
see Warner-Chappell Music

Big Life Music (BMI)
see Warner-Chappell Music

Big Pig Music
see Warner-Chappell Music

Big Tooth Music Corp. (ASCAP)
see Chrysalis Music Group

Big Will (ASCAP)
see Polygram Music Publishing Inc.

Bilv (BMI)
see Famous Music Corp.

Binky Music (BMI)
see Longitude Music

Black Bull Music (BMI)
Att: Stevland Morris
4616 Magnolia Blvd.
Burbank, California 91505

Black Ice Music (BMI)
see Flyte Tyme Tunes

Blackened (BMI)
c/o Prager & Fenton
12424 Wilshire Blvd., Ste. 1000
Los Angeles, California 90025

Bludgeon Riffola Music (ASCAP)
see Zomba Music

Blue Dandelion (BMI)
see EMI Music Publishing

Blue Ink (BMI)
see Tommy Boy Music

Blue Lake Music (BMI)
see Terrace Music

Blue Saint Music (ASCAP)
see Famous Music Corp.

Blue Turtle
see Magnetic Music Publishing Co.

BMG Music (ASCAP)
1133 Sixth Avenue
New York, New York 10036

BMG Songs Inc. (ASCAP)
1133 Avenue of the Americas
New York, New York 10036

Bon Jovi Publishing (ASCAP)
see Polygram Music Publishing Inc.

Boobie Loo (BMI)
see Warner-Chappell Music

Bovina Music, Inc. (ASCAP)
c/o Mae Attaway
330 W. 56th Street, Apt. 12F
New York, New York 10019

Bridgeport Music Inc. (BMI)
c/o Sam Peterer Music
530 E. 76th St.
New York, New York 10021

Brittlesse (ASCAP)
see Me Good Music

Brockman Enterprises Inc. (ASCAP)
Leibren Music Division
c/o Jess S. Morgan & Co., Inc.
6420 Wilshire Blvd., 19th Fl.
Los Angeles, California 90048

Brooklyn Based (ASCAP)
see EMI Music Publishing

Bobby Brown (ASCAP)
see EMI Music Publishing

Brown Dog (BMI)
see Warner-Chappell Music

Bruised Oranges (BMI)
4121 Wilshire Blvd., Ste. 5204
Los Angeles, California 10017

Brupo (BMI)
see Warner-Chappell Music

Budget Music (BMI)
c/o Mietus Copyright Management
P.O. Box 432
Union, New Jersey 07083

Bug Music (BMI)
Bug Music Group
6777 Hollywood Blvd., 9th Fl.
Hollywood, California 90028

Burbank Plaza Music (ASCAP)
see EMI Music Publishing

Gary Burr Music (BMI)
see Tree Publishing Co., Inc.

# C

Cameo Appearance by Ramses (ASCAP)
see MCA Music

Camp Songs Music (BMI)
see BMG Music

Canopy Music Inc. (ASCAP)
see White Oak Songs

Careers-BMG
see BMG Music

Castle Street (ASCAP)
1025 16th Ave. S., Ste. 102
Nashville, Tennessee 37212

Cats on the Prowl (ASCAP)
6247 Arlington Ave.
Los Angeles, California 90043

Champaign House (BMI)
see Del Sounds Music

Champion Music (BMI)
see Sony Tree

Chappell & Co., Inc. (ASCAP)
see Warner-Chappell Music

Charm Trap Music (BMI)
see EMI Music Publishing

Chekerman (BMI)
see Warner-Chappell Music

Chelcait Music (BMI)
6124 Selma Avenue
Hollywood, California 90028

Cherry Lane Music Co. (ASCAP)
110 Midland Avenue
Port Chester, New York 10573

Christian Burial Music (ASCAP)
c/o The New York End Ltd.
29 W. 65th St.
New York, New York 10023

Frank Christian Music (BMI)
c/o Michael Lessor
162 E. 64th St.
New York, New York 10021

Chrysalis Music Group (ASCAP)
9255 Sunset Blvd.
Los Angeles, California 90069

Chyskillz (ASCAP)
see EMI Music Publishing

Cisum Ludes (ASCAP)
see Next Plateau Entertainment

City Beat Music (ASCAP)
110-20 73rd Rd., Apt. 5N
Forest Hills, New York 11375

Clannad Music Ltd. (Ireland)
Address Unavailable

Cliofine (BMI)
see Hit & Run Music

CMI America (ASCAP)
1102 17th Ave. S.
Nashville, Tennessee 37212

Coal Dust West (BMI)
c/o Zifrin, Brittenham & Branca
2121 Avenue of the Stars, Suite 320
0
Los Angeles, California 90067

Leonard Cohen Stranger Music Inc. (BMI)
c/o Keller Lynch
146 W. 75th Street
New York, New York 10023

Colby Music, Inc. (ASCAP)
c/o Samuel Jesse Buzzell
460 Park Avenue
New York, New York 10022

Coleision Music (BMI)
see EMI Music Publishing

Colgems-EMI Music (ASCAP)
see EMI Music Publishing

Tom Collins Music Corp. (BMI)
25 Music Sq. W
Nashville, Tennessee 37203

Phil Collins (ASCAP)
see Hit & Run Music

Colored Folks Music (ASCAP)
203 Martin's Lane
Rockville, Maryland 20850

Colpix (BMI)
see Sony Music

Conrad Music (ASCAP)
c/o The Goodman Group
488 Madison Ave., 5th Fl.
New York, New York 10022

Controversy Music (ASCAP)
c/o Manatt, Phelps, Rothenberg
Att: Lee Phillips
11355 W. Olympic Blvd.
Los Angeles, California 90064

Copyright Control (ASCAP)
see Bug Music

Core Music Publishing (BMI)
c/o Oak Manor
Box 1000
Oak Ridges, Ontario
Canada

Could Be Music (BMI)
see MCA Music

Country Road Music Inc. (BMI)
c/o Gelfand, Rennert & Feldman
Att: Babbie Green
1880 Century Park, E., No. 900
Los Angeles, California 90067

CPMK (BMI)
see Zomba Music

CPZ (ASCAP)
see Zomba Music

Crash (BMI)
see Jamie Music Publishing Co.

Crooked Fingers (ASCAP)
see AGF Music Ltd.

Mike Curb Productions (BMI)
948 Tourmaline Dr.
Newbury Park, California 91220

Cypress Phunky (ASCAP)
see MCA Music

# List of Publishers

## D

Dandelion Music Co. (BMI)
see Jamie Music Publishing Co.

D.A.R.P. Music (ASCAP)
see Diva One

Dave & Darlene Music (ASCAP)
c/o Evan Dando
79 Minot Street
Dorchester, Massachusetts 02122

De Burgo (ASCAP)
see Polygram Music Publishing Inc.

Deep Groove (BMI)
see Protoons Inc.

Deerfield Court Music (BMI)
see Sony Tree

Del Sounds Music (BMI)
c/o Happy Valley Music
1 Camp Street
Cambridge, Massachusetts 02140

Deshane (ASCAP)
see Zomba Music

Deswing Mob (ASCAP)
see EMI Music Publishing

Walt Disney Music (ASCAP)
500 S. Buena Vista Street
Burbank, California 91521

Diva One (ASCAP)
Gelfand, Rennert & Feldman
c/o Michael Bivens
1880 Century Park East, Ste. 900
Los Angeles, California 90067

Dixie Stars Music (ASCAP)
see Zomba Music

Dog Dream (ASCAP)
Box 483
Newton Centre, Massachusetts 02159

Doll Face (BMI)
see Jobete Music Co., Inc.

Donril Music (ASCAP)
see Zomba House

Dovan Music (ASCAP)
Box 33079
Houston, Texas 77233

Dresden China Music (ASCAP)
see Warner-Chappell Music

Dub Notes
23 E. Lancaster Ave.
Ardmore, Pennsylvania 19003

Mike Dunn (ASCAP)
see Colby Music, Inc.

Dyad Music, Ltd. (BMI)
c/o Mason & Co.
75 Rockefeller Plaza
New York, New York 10019

## E

E/A Music (BMI)
see Warner-Chappell Music

Eaglewood (BMI)
c/o Irving Music
1358 N. La Brea
Hollywood, California 90028

East Jesus (ASCAP)
see Warner-Chappell Music

Ecaf (BMI)
see Sony Music

Edisto Music (BMI)
see Sony Tree

Edition (ASCAP)
see Warner-Chappell Music

Eel Pie Music (ASCAP)
see Towser Tunes Inc.

Eighth Nerve (BMI)
see Red Brazos

Elegant Mule (ASCAP)
c/o Meibach Epstein Reiss & Regis
680 5th Ave.
New York, New York 10019

Brian Elliot (ASCAP)
see Great Honesty Music Inc.

Emerald River (BMI)
see MCA Music

EMI-April Music (ASCAP)
see EMI Music Publishing

EMI-Blackwood Music Inc. (BMI)
see EMI Music Publishing

EMI Music Publishing
1290 Avenue of the Americas
New York, New York 10104

EMI Songs Ltd.
see EMI Music Publishing

EMI-10 (ASCAP)
see EMI Music Publishing

EMI U Catalogue (ASCAP)
see EMI Music Publishing

EMI Unart Catalogue
Address Unavailable

EMI-Virgin (ASCAP)
see EMI Music Publishing

End of August (ASCAP)
c/o William Terry
3305 Dunn St.
Smyrna, Georgia 30080

End of Music (BMI)
see EMI Music Publishing

Englishtown (BMI)
see Warner-Chappell Music

Ensign Music (BMI)
see Famous Music Corp.

Essential Music (ASCAP)
see Warner-Chappell Music

Estefan Music (ASCAP)
see Foreign Imported

Ethyl (ASCAP)
see MCA Music

Exaskeletal (BMI)
see Warner-Chappell Music


**F**

Faith Hope and Charity (BMI)
see Warner-Chappell Music

Famous Music Corp. (ASCAP)
15 Columbus Circle
New York, New York 10023

Father MC (ASCAP)
see EMI Music Publishing

Fiddleback (BMI)
see Valando Group

Flavor Unit Music (ASCAP)
see Almo/Irving

Floated Music (ASCAP)
see EMI Music Publishing

Flow Tech (BMI)
see EMI Music Publishing

Fluxin Music (ASCAP)
see BMG Music

Flying Dutchman (BMI)
c/o Copyright Management Inc.
P.O. Box 110873
Nashville, Tennessee 37211

Flyte Tyme Tunes (ASCAP)
c/o Avant Garde Music Publishing
9229 Sunset Blvd., Suite 311
Los Angeles, California 90069

Foreign Imported (BMI)
8921 S.W. Tenth Terrace
Miami, Florida 33174

# List of Publishers

Forerunner Music (ASCAP)
1308 16th Ave. S
Nashville, Tennessee 37212

Foreshadow Songs, Inc. (BMI)
P.O. Box 120657
Nashville, Tennessee 37212

Forrest Hills Music Inc. (BMI)
1609 Hawkins Street
Nashville, Tennessee 37203

Forty Floors Up (ASCAP)
see Zomba Music

Four Knights Music Co. (BMI)
see MCA Music

4MW (ASCAP)
see Burbank Plaza Music

Frabensha (ASCAP)
see MCA Music

Freedom Songs (BMI)
see Warner-Chappell Music

Freejunket Music (ASCAP)
c/o Salter Street Music
123 El Paseo
Santa Barbara, California 93101

Full Keel (ASCAP)
4450 Lakeside Dr., Ste. 200
Burbank, California 91505

Full Nelson (BMI)
see Windswept Pacific

# G

Al Gallico Music Corp. (BMI)
9301 Wilshire, Ste. 311
Beverly Hills, California 90210

Gangsta Boogie (ASCAP)
see Warner-Chappell Music

Garden Court Music Co. (ASCAP)
Box 1098
Alexandria, Ontario K0C 1A0
Canada

Gasoline Alley Music (BMI)
see MCA Music

Get Into Magic (ASCAP)
see Warner-Chappell Music

Getarealjob Music (ASCAP)
see EMI Music Publishing

G.G. Loves Music (BMI)
see Warner-Chappell Music

Ghatti Music (ASCAP)
see Warner-Chappell Music

Ghetto Gospel (BMI)
see Warner-Chappell Music

Gigolo Chez Publishing (BMI)
Box 6367
North Augusta, Georgia 29841

Giro Productions (BMI)
3832 Lake Aire Dr.
Nashville, Tennessee 37217

Gladys Music (ASCAP)
see Hudson Bay Music

Seymour Glass (BMI)
see EMI Music Publishing

GLG Two (BMI)
13624 Sherman Way, #450
Van Nuys, California 91405

Golden Reed Music (ASCAP)
Box 121081
1013 16th Avenue S.
Nashville, Tennessee 37202

Golden Withers (ASCAP)
see Warner-Chappell Music

Gone Gator Music (ASCAP)
c/o Zeiderman, Oberman & Assoc.
500 Sepulveda Blvd., Ste. 500
Los Angeles, California 90049

Grabbing Hands (ASCAP)
see EMI Music Publishing

Gradington Music (ASCAP)
  see MCA Music

Great Honesty Music Inc.
  P.O. Box 547
  Larkspur, California 94977

Great Walrus Ltd. (ASCAP)
  see Warner-Chappell Music

Green Skirt Music (BMI)
  see Kear Music

Green Snow (ASCAP)
  see Warner-Chappell Music

Ground Control (BMI)
  see EMI Music Publishing

# H
Hamstein Music (BMI)
  c/o Bill Ham
  P.O. Box 19647
  Houston, Texas 77024

Hang Onto Your Publishing (BMI)
  see Bug Music

Harrick Music Inc. (BMI)
  see Longitude Music

Harris Onyx (ASCAP)
  see EMI Music Publishing

Juliana Hatfield (BMI)
  see Zomba Music

Haverstraw (ASCAP)
  506 3rd St.
  Brooklyn, New York 11215

Heathalee (BMI)
  see EMI Music Publishing

Heavy Melon (ASCAP)
  9255 Sunset Blvd., Ste. 620
  Los Angeles, California 90069

Hee Bee Dooinit
  Address Unavailable

HEG Music (ASCAP)
  6381 Hollywood Blvd., Ste. 5250
  Hollywood, California 90028

Hi-Frost
  Address Unavailable

Hidden Music (BMI)
  see Hit & Run Music

Hidden Pun (BMI)
  1841 Broadway
  New York, New York 10023

Himownself's Music Co. (ASCAP)
  see AMR

Hip City
  Address unavailable

Hit & Run Music (ASCAP)
  1841 Broadway, Suite 411
  New York, New York 10023

Hot Head Ltd. (England)
  Address unavailable

House Jam (ASCAP)
  see Zomba Music

Harlan Howard Songs (BMI)
  59 Music Square, W.
  Nashville, Tennessee 37203

Howlin' Hits Music (ASCAP)
  P.O. Box 19647
  Houston, Texas 77224

Hudmar Publishing Co., Inc. (BMI)
  c/o Fitzgerald/Hartley
  50 W. Main
  Ventura, California 93001

Hudson Bay Music (BMI)
  1619 Broadway
  New York, New York 10019

Human Boy Music (ASCAP)
  see Warner-Chappell Music

# List of Publishers

## I

ICM (ASCAP)
see Warner-Chappell Music

I'll Hit You Back (BMI)
see EMI Music Publishing

I'll Hit You Back (BMI)
see WB Music

Imago Songs (ASCAP)
152 W. 57th Street
New York, New York 10019

Impulsive Music (ASCAP)
see EMI Music Publishing

In Stereo (ASCAP)
c/o Audley Freed
410 Park Ave.
New York, New York 10022

Index Music (ASCAP)
see Warner-Chappell Music

Innocent Bystander Music (ASCAP)
207 1/2 First Avenue S.
Seattle, Washington 98104

Interscope Pearl (BMI)
see Warner-Chappell Music

Intersong, USA Inc. (ASCAP)
see Warner-Chappell Music

Irving Music Inc. (BMI)
1358 N. La Brea
Hollywood, California 90028

C. Isaak (ASCAP)
see Great Honesty Music Inc.

Chris Isaak Music Publishing (ASCAP)
P.O. Box 547
Larkspur, California 94939

Island Music (BMI)
6525 Sunset Blvd.
Los Angeles, California 90028

Issac (ASCAP)
see Chris Isaak Music Publishing

Iza (BMI)
see Clyde Otis Music

## J

Jamie Music Publishing Co. (BMI)
2055 Richmond St.
Philadelphia, Pennsylvania 19125

Patrix Janus (ASCAP)
119 17th Ave. S
Nashville, Tennessee 37203

Jazz Merchant Music (ASCAP)
see Zomba Music

Jazzy Jeff & Fresh Prince (ASCAP)
see Zomba Music

Jeffix Music Co. (ASCAP)
c/o William Jeffery
5143 Village Green
Los Angeles, California 90016

Jello-R-Us (ASCAP)
see Chrysalis Music Group

Jessie Joe (BMI)
Address Unavailable

Jimmie Fun (BMI)
see EMI Music Publishing

JMV Music Inc. (ASCAP)
see CMI America

Jobete Music Co., Inc. (ASCAP)
Att: Erlinda N. Barrios
6255 Sunset Blvd., Suite 1600
Hollywood, California 90028

Jondora Music (BMI)
Tenth & Parker Streets
Berkeley, California 94710

Jones Fall Music (BMI)
see EMI Music Publishing

Lucy Jones Music (BMI)
see Warner-Chappell Music

Patrick Joseph (BMI)
  119 17th Ave. S
  Nashville, Tennessee 37203

Joshuasongs (BMI)
  see EMI Music Publishing

Judgemental Music (BMI)
  see Bug Music

Julien (ASCAP)
  see Polygram Music Publishing Inc.

Jumping Cat Music (ASCAP)
  see Write Treatage Music

# K

K-Man (BMI)
  see Sony Music

Kakalaka Music (BMI)
  see Warner-Chappell Music

Kander & Ebb Inc. (BMI)
  see Valando Group

Katsback (ASCAP)
  see Warner-Chappell Music

Kear Music (BMI)
  1635 N. Cahuenga Blvd.
  Los Angeles, California 90028

R. Kelly Music (BMI)
  see Zomba Music

Kenny G (BMI)
  c/o Turner Management Group
  3500 W. Olive St., Ste. 770
  Burbank, California 91505

King Kino (ASCAP)
  see Warner-Chappell Music

Kole, Moke & Noke (BMI)
  Box 724677
  Atlanta, Georgia 31139

# L

La Familia (BMI)
  see Almo/Irving

L.A. Jay (ASCAP)
  see Polygram Music Publishing Inc.

Lamartine (ASCAP)
  see Lost Lake Arts Music

Large Giant (ASCAP)
  see Sony Music

Latino Buggerveil Music (ASCAP)
  see Warner-Chappell Music

Lazarus Ltd. (England)
  Address Unavailable

Let's Have Lunch Music (ASCAP)
  see Polygram Music Publishing Inc.

Lev-a-Tunes (ASCAP)
  see Bug Music

LFR Music (ASCAP)
  see Warner-Chappell Music

Lillybilly
  see Bug Music

Lilyac (ASCAP)
  c/o Patrick Rains & Assoc.
  9034 Sunset Blvd., Ste. 250
  Los Angeles, California 90069

Linda's Boys Music (BMI)
  see WB Music

Linde Manor Publishing Co. (BMI)
  Rte. 1, Lakeview Dr.
  Hermitage, Tennessee 37076

Little Big Town Music (BMI)
  see Jessie Joe

Little Reata (BMI)
  see Irving Music Inc.

Little Roz (BMI)
  see EMI Music Publishing

Loc'ed Out (ASCAP)
see Polygram Music Publishing Inc.

Loggy Bayou Music (ASCAP)
1303 Saturn Drive
Nashville, Tennessee 37217

Longitude Music (BMI)
c/o Windswept Pacific Entertainment
Co.
4450 Lakeside Drive, Suite 200
Burbank, California 91505

Lost Lake Arts Music (ASCAP)
c/o Windham Hill Records
75 Willow Rd.
Menlo Park, California 94025

Love Tribe Music (ASCAP)
see MCA Music

Ludakris (ASCAP)
see BMG Music

Luersrika (BMI)
see Almo/Irving

Luna Mist Music (BMI)
c/o Laura Bianchini
Box 2865
Danbury, Connecticut 06813

# M

Madfly Music (ASCAP)
see Warner-Chappell Music

Madwoman (BMI)
see Polygram Music Publishing Inc.

Magnetic Music Publishing Co. (ASCAP)
5 Jones St., Apt. 4
New York, New York 10014

Magnified (ASCAP)
see Warner-Chappell Music

Major Bob Music (ASCAP)
see Sony Cross Keys Publishing Co. Inc.

Mama Guitar (ASCAP)
see Polygram Music Publishing Inc.

E. B. Marks Music Corp. (BMI)
see Alley Music

Matak Music (ASCAP)
see MCA Music

Mattie Ruth Musick (ASCAP)
1010 16th Ave. South
Nashville, Tennessee 37212

Maverick (ASCAP)
see Warner-Chappell Music

M.C. Shan (ASCAP)
50-02 94th St.
Elmhurst, New York 11373

MCA Music (ASCAP)
Division of MCA Inc.
445 Park Avenue
New York, New York 10022

McBroom Music (BMI)
Box 430
Port Chester, New York 10573

Me Good Music (ASCAP)
see Almo Music Corp.

Medad (BMI)
see Almo/Irving

Megasongs
see BMG Music

Mercy Kersey (BMI)
see Almo/Irving

Miching Mallecko (BMI)
see Bug Music

Mighty Nice Music (BMI)
see Polygram Music Publishing Inc.

Mijac Music (BMI)
see Warner-Chappell Music

Millhouse Music (BMI)
see Polygram Music Publishing Inc.

Miss Bessie Music (ASCAP)
9247 Alden Drive
Los Angeles, California 90210

Miss Pammy's (ASCAP)
see AMR

Mr. Bolton's Music (BMI)
c/o David Feinstein
120 E. 34th Street, Suite 7F
New York, New York 10011

MLE Music (ASCAP)
see Almo Music Corp.

Moebetoblame Music (BMI)
1990 Bundy Drive
Los Angeles, California 90025

Momentum Ltd. (BMI)
1201 Larrabee St.
Los Angeles, California 90069

Monosteri Music (ASCAP)
c/o Zachary Glickman Artist
Management
19301 Ventura Blvd., Suite 205
Tarzana, California 91356

Moo Music (ASCAP)
see Dave & Darlene Music

Moon Junction (ASCAP)
see EMI Music Publishing

Moonwindow Music (ASCAP)
c/o David Ellingson
737 Latimer Road
Santa Monica, California 90402

Mopage (BMI)
334 3rd Ave. Sn
Franklin, Tennessee 37064

Gary Morris Music (ASCAP)
c/o Cooper, Epstein & Hurewitz
342 Maple Dr.
Beverly Hills, California 90210

Mother Bertha Music, Inc. (BMI)
686 S. Arroyo Pkwy., Penthouse
Pasadena, California 91105

Motor Jam (ASCAP)
Box 503
Bayside, New York 11361

Mow B' Jow Music (BMI)
see Sony Songs

MPL Communications Inc. (ASCAP)
c/o Lee Eastman
39 W. 54th Street
New York, New York 10019

Mumblety Peg (BMI)
see BMG Music

Murrah (BMI)
1025 16th Ave. South, Ste. 102
P.O. Box 121623
Nashville, Tennessee 37212

Museum Steps Music (ASCAP)
Gelfand, Rennert & Feldman
6 E. 43rd St.
New York, New York 10017

Music by Candlelight (ASCAP)
see Peer-Southern Organization

Music Corp. of America (BMI)
see MCA Music

Music of the World (BMI)
8857 W. Olympic Blvd.
Beverly Hills, California 90210

# N

N-The Water Publishing (ASCAP)
12337 Jones Road
Suite 100
Houston, Texas 77070

Naughty (ASCAP)
see Jobete Music Co., Inc.

Nelana Music (BMI)
c/o Fishbach & Fishbach
1925 Century Park, E., Suite 1260
Los Angeles, California 90067

Ness, Nitty & Capone (ASCAP)
see EMI-April Music

Neve Welt Musikverlag (Germany)
Address Unavailable

New Clarion (ASCAP)
Box 121081
Nashville, Tennessee 37212

New Hayes Music (ASCAP)
see Don Schlitz Music

New Nonpariel (BMI)
see Warner-Chappell Music

New Perspective Publishing, Inc. (ASCAP)
see Avant Garde Music

New Songs (ASCAP)
see Polygram Music Publishing Inc.

Wood Newton (ASCAP)
see AMR

Next Plateau Entertainment (ASCAP)
1650 Broadway
New York, New York 10019

Nick-O-Val Music (ASCAP)
254 W. 72nd Street, Suite 1A
New York, New York 10023

Night Garden Music (BMI)
see Warner-Chappell Music

No Dooze (ASCAP)
see Chrysalis Music Group

No Fences Music (BMI)
see EMI Music Publishing

Nocturnal Eclipse Music (BMI)
see Dyad Music, Ltd.

Nomad-Noman (BMI)
see Warner-Chappell Music

NYM (ASCAP)
5036 Medina Road
Woodland Hills, California 91364

# O

O/B/O/Itself (ASCAP)
see Almo/Irving

O-Tex Music (BMI)
see Zomba Music

Oakfield Avenue Music Ltd. (BMI)
c/o David Gotterer
Mason & Co.
75 Rockefeller Plaza, Suite 1800
New York, New York 10019

October Project (ASCAP)
see Famous Music Corp.

The Old Professor's (ASCAP)
see EMI Music Publishing

One Four Three
see Warner-Chappell Music

Ronnie Onyx (BMI)
see MCA Music

Open Window Music Co. (BMI)
c/o Gudvi Chapnick, Esq.
15250 Ventura Blvd., Ste. 900
Sherman Oaks, California 91403

Orbisongs (ASCAP)
see EMI-April Music

Clyde Otis Music (BMI)
Box 325
Englewood, New Jersey 07631

# P

Pac Jam Publishing (BMI)
see Warner-Chappell Music

Pearl White (BMI)
see EMI Music Publishing

Peer-Southern Organization (ASCAP)
810 7th Ave.
New York, New York 10019

Pentagon Lipservices Real World (BMI)
see Hit & Run Music

Perfect (ASCAP)
see Zomba Music

Period Music
  see Zomba Music

Pete Rock (ASCAP)
  see Protoons Inc.

Peter's Cathedral
  4 Hardie Way
  Bela Cynwyd, Pennsylvania 19004

Pickled Fish Music (ASCAP)
  see Write Treatage Music

Pink Smoke Music (BMI)
  see EMI Music Publishing

PKM Music (ASCAP)
  Box 5807
  Englewood, New Jersey 07631

Placid Music Corp. (BMI)
  see Warner-Chappell Music

Platinum Plateau (ASCAP)
  see Almo/Irving

Playful Music (BMI)
  see Warner-Chappell Music

Playhard Music (ASCAP)
  2434 Main Street
  Santa Monica, California 90405

Polygram International (ASCAP)
  see Polygram Music Publishing Inc.

Polygram Music Publishing Inc. (ASCAP)
  Att: Brian Kelleher
  c/o Polygram Records Inc.
  810 Seventh Avenue
  New York, New York 10019

Ponder Heart Music (BMI)
  see Almo Music Corp.

Possibilities (ASCAP)
  see EMI Music Publishing

Post Oak (BMI)
  see Sony Tree

Pressmancherry (ASCAP)
  see Warner-Chappell Music

Pressmancherryblossom (BMI)
  see Warner-Chappell Music

Hugh Prestwood (BMI)
  see BMG Music

PRI Music (ASCAP)
  see Polygram Music Publishing Inc.

Promuse (BMI)
  see Protoons Inc.

Prophet Sharing Music (ASCAP)
  4049 Edenhurst Avenue
  Los Angeles, California 90039

Prosthytumes (ASCAP)
  see HEG Music

Protoons Inc. (ASCAP)
  c/o Profile Records Inc.
  Att: Cory Robins
  740 Broadway, 7th Fl.
  New York, New York 10003

PSO Ltd. (ASCAP)
  see Peer-Southern Organization

## Q

Queen Latifah (ASCAP)
  see MCA Music

Queen Music Ltd. (BMI)
  see EMI Music Publishing

Quick Time (BMI)
  see EMI Music Publishing

## R

R-Bar-P (ASCAP)
  see Polygram Music Publishing Inc.

Ram-Page Publishing Ltd. (BMI)
  see Triple Star Music

Ramal Music Co. (BMI)
  5999 Bear Creek Rd. No. 304
  Bedford Heights, Ohio 44146

Ranch Rock Music (ASCAP)
see Warner-Chappell Music

Ranger Bob Music (ASCAP)
54 Music Sq. E
Nashville, Tennessee 37203

Rap and More Music (BMI)
c/o Manatt, Phelps, Rothenberg & Ph
ilips
11355 W. Olympic Blvd.
Los Angeles, California 90064

Reach Around Music (BMI)
c/o Keith Spaulding
1560 West Bay Area Blvd., Ste. 105
Friendsweed, Texas 77546

Real World Music (BMI)
see Hit & Run Music

Realsongs (ASCAP)
Attn: Diane Warren
6363 Sunset Blvd., Ste. 806-08
Hollywood, California 90028

Red Brazos (BMI)
Box 163870
Austin, Texas 78716

Rejoice (BMI)
see Polygram Music Publishing Inc.

Rella Music Corp. (BMI)
see Warner-Chappell Music

RET Music Inc. (ASCAP)
c/o Victor Marquez
1 CNN Center, 8th Fl.
Box 105366
Atlanta, Georgia 30348

Rev (ASCAP)
see Polygram Music Publishing Inc.

Reyshell (BMI)
see Warner-Chappell Music

Rightsong Music (BMI)
see Warner-Chappell Music

Risque Situe Music (BMI)
see Warner-Chappell Music

Rock Pop Music (BMI)
c/o Ian Lewis
55 N.W. 192nd St.
Miami, Florida 33169

Rondor Music Inc. (ASCAP)
see Almo Music Corp.

Rose Hips Music
P.O. Drawer S17
Dickson, Tennessee 37055

Rubber Band Music, Inc. (BMI)
c/o Gelfand, Breslaver, Rennert
and Feldman
1800 Century Park, E., Suite 900
Los Angeles, California 90067

Rush Groove (ASCAP)
see Protoons Inc.

Rush Town Music Assoc. Labels (ASCAP)
652 Broadway, 3rd Fl.
New York, New York 10012

Michael Rutherford Music (ASCAP)
see Hit & Run Music

Rye Songs (BMI)
see Sony Music

# S

Saba Seven Music (BMI)
see Famous Music Corp.

Saints Alive (ASCAP)
see Warner-Chappell Music

Saja Music Co. (BMI)
see Warner-Chappell Music

Salafa Ltd. (England)
Address Unavailable

Kevin Savigar (ASCAP)
see Almo Music Corp.

SBK Songs (BMI)
  see EMI Music Publishing

Don Schlitz Music (ASCAP)
  see Almo Music Corp.

Schmemetone (ASCAP)
  see Chrysalis Music Group

Scratch 'N' Source (ASCAP)
  see Zomba Music

Scred Songs
  see AGF Music Ltd.

Screen Gems-EMI Music Inc. (BMI)
  6255 Sunset Blvd., 12th Fl.
  Hollywood, California 90028

Scribing C-Ment Music (ASCAP)
  see Write Treatage Music

Seagrape Music Inc. (BMI)
  c/o Jess S. Morgan & Co.
  5750 Wilshire Blvd., Ste. 590
  Los Angeles, California 90036

John Sebastian Music (BMI)
  c/o Goldfine, CPA
  225 W. 34th St.
  New York, New York 10122

Second Generation Rooney Tunes (BMI)
  see MCA Music

See the Light (BMI)
  see Cherry Lane Music Co.

Seldak Music Corp. (ASCAP)
  155 E. 55th St., Ste. 6H
  New York, New York 10022

Seven Angels (BMI)
  see Sony Tree

Seventh Son Music (ASCAP)
  Box 158717
  Nashville, Tennessee 37215

Sextunes Music (ASCAP)
  see MCA Music

Shanice 4U (ASCAP)
  see Warner-Chappell Music

Shepsongs (ASCAP)
  see MCA Music

Sierra Home (ASCAP)
  see AMR

Silver Angel Music (ASCAP)
  see Playhard Music

Silver Fiddle (ASCAP)
  c/o Segel & Goldman Inc.
  9200 Sunset Blvd., Suite 1000
  Los Angeles, California 90069

Silver State (ASCAP)
  see Warner-Chappell Music

Skull Music (BMI)
  c/o Mac Rebennack
  1995 Broadway
  New York, New York 10023

Sky Garden Music (ASCAP)
  see Peer-Southern Organization

Sleeping Son Music Inc. (BMI)
  see EMI Music Publishing

Slow Dog Music (BMI)
  c/o Geronimo
  1 Camp St., Ste. 2
  Cambridge, Massachusetts 02140

Smokin' Sounds (ASCAP)
  see EMI Music Publishing

Smooth Flowin' (ASCAP)
  see Warner-Chappell Music

Snowden Music (ASCAP)
  Box 11512th Street
  Purdys, New York 10578

So So Def Music (ASCAP)
  see EMI Music Publishing

Song-a-Tron (BMI)
  see Sony Tree

Songs of Iris
see Forerunner Music

Songs of Polygram (BMI)
see Polygram Music Publishing Inc.

Songwriters Ink (BMI)
see Forrest Hills Music Inc.

Sony Cross Keys Publishing Co. Inc.
c/o Donna Hilley
P.O. Box 1273
Nashville, Tennessee 37202

Sony Music (ASCAP)
550 Madison Ave.
New York, New York 10022

Sony Songs (BMI)
see Sony Music

Sony Tree (BMI)
8 Music Square W.
Nashville, Tennessee 37202

Sony Tunes (ASCAP)
see Sony Music

Sophie's Choice Music (BMI)
1705 Warfield Drive
Nashville, Tennessee 37215

Soul Assassins Music (ASCAP)
see T-Boy Music Publishing Co., Inc.

Sound Mind & Body (BMI)
see Warner-Chappell Music

Southern Music Publishing Co., Inc. (ASCAP)
Att: Ralph Peer, II
1740 Broadway
New York, New York 10019

Special Rider Music (ASCAP)
P.O. Box 860, Cooper Sta.
New York, New York 10276

Bruce Springsteen Publishing (ASCAP)
c/o Jon Landau Management, Inc.
Att: Barbara Carr
136 E. 57th Street, No. 1202
New York, New York 10021

Sprint (BMI)
Address Unavailable

Spyder Mae (ASCAP)
see Chrysalis Music Group

Square West (ASCAP)
see Howlin' Hits Music

Starry Plough Music (BMI)
31-33 Mercer Street
Apt. 2C
New York, New York 10013

Stay Straight (BMI)
see Hit & Run Music

Stazybo Music (BMI)
c/o Will Bratton
611 Broadway, Ste. 422
New York, New York 10012

Step Up Front (ASCAP)
see Warner-Chappell Music

Jeff Stevens (BMI)
see Warner-Chappell Music

S.T.M. Music (BMI)
see Warner-Chappell Music

Stone Agate Music (ASCAP)
see Jobete Music Co., Inc.

Stone Diamond Music (BMI)
see Jobete Music Co., Inc.

Stone Jam Music (ASCAP)
see Warner-Chappell Music

Stonebridge Music (ASCAP)
The Bicycle Music Co.
8075 W. Third Street, Suite 400
Los Angeles, California 90048

Story Songs Ltd. (ASCAP)
83 Green St.
Huntington, New York 11743

Straight Cash (BMI)
see EMI Music Publishing

Streamline Moderne (BMI)
see Warner-Chappell Music

Street Knowledge (BMI)
see Unichappell Music Inc.

Stuck in the Throat (ASCAP)
see Famous Music Corp.

Succubus Music (ASCAP)
see Warner-Chappell Music

Suge (BMI)
see Sony Music

Suolabaf Music (BMI)
see Towser Tunes Inc.

Super Supa Songs (ASCAP)
see MCA Music

Swag Song Music (ASCAP)
5 Bigelow Street
Cambridge, Massachusetts 02129

Swallow Turn Music (ASCAP)
c/o Manatt, Phelps, Rothenberg & Ph
illips
11355 W. Olympic Blvd.
Los Angeles, California 90064

Keith Sweat Music (ASCAP)
see Warner-Chappell Music

# T

T-Boy Music Publishing Co., Inc. (ASCAP)
c/o Lipservices
1841 Broadway
New York, New York 10023

T-Ray (BMI)
see MCA Music

Tallyrand Music (ASCAP)
see Stonebridge Music

Taosongs Music
see MCA Music

Taste Auction (BMI)
see Warner-Chappell Music

Taylor Rhodes Music (ASCAP)
210 Lauderdale Road
Nashville, Tennessee 37205

Tee Girl Music (BMI)
see Tommy Boy Music

Terrace Music (BMI)
Box 239
Las Vegas, Nevada 87701

Texas Wedge (ASCAP)
11 Music Square East
Nashville, Tennessee 37212

Thanxamillion (BMI)
see Sony Tree

Third and Lex (BMI)
see Tommy Boy Music

This Big (ASCAP)
see Sony Music

Thriller Miller Music (ASCAP)
9034 Sunset Blvd., Suite 250
Los Angeles, California 90069

Tillis Tunes (BMI)
809 18th Ave. S
Nashville, Tennessee 37203

Toe Knee Hangs (ASCAP)
see HEG Music

Tokeco (BMI)
see Polygram Music Publishing Inc.

Tommy Boy Music (BMI)
902 Broadway
New York, New York 10010

Tommy Jymi, Inc. (BMI)
c/o Dennis Katz, Esq.
845 Third Avenue
New York, New York 10022

Tony! Toni! Tone! (ASCAP)
see PRI Music

Too Strong (BMI)
see Famous Music Corp.

# List of Publishers

Top Billin (ASCAP)
see EMI Music Publishing

Tortured Artist (ASCAP)
see Sony Music

Towser Tunes Inc. (BMI)
c/o Ina Lea Meibach
Meibach & Epstein
680 5th Ave.
New York, New York 10019

Tradition Music Co. (BMI)
see Bug Music

Tranquility Base Songs (ASCAP)
see Warner-Chappell Music

Traveling Zoo (ASCAP)
see Beginner Music

Tree Publishing Co., Inc. (BMI)
P.O. Box 1273
Nashville, Tennessee 37203

Tri Ryche (BMI)
see Sony Songs

Trio Music Co., Inc. (BMI)
c/o Leiber & Stoller
9000 Sunset Blvd., Ste. 1107
Loa Angeles, California 90045

Triple Star Music (BMI)
see EMI Music Publishing

Troutman's (BMI)
Lefrak-Moelis Ent. Group
40 W. 57th St., Ste. 510
New York, New York 10019

Trunksong Music (BMI)
c/o The Shokatt Company, Ltd.
340 W. 55th Street, Suite 1A
New York, New York 10019

Trycep Publishing Co. (BMI)
c/o John P. Kellog, Esq.
33 Public Square, No. 810
Cleveland, Ohio 44113

TSP Music, Inc.
1875 Century Park, E., Suite 700
Los Angeles, California 90067

Two Tuff-Enuff Music (BMI)
see Almo Music Corp.

## U

U/A Music, Inc. (ASCAP)
Metro-Goldwyn-Mayer Inc
Attn: Music Dept.
10000 W. Washington Blvd.
Ste. 3021
Culver City, California 90232

Unart Music Corp. (BMI)
see United Artists Music Co., Inc.

Uncle Ronnie's Music (ASCAP)
see EMI Music Publishing

Undercurrent (ASCAP)
see Warner-Chappell Music

Unichappell Music Inc. (BMI)
see Warner-Chappell Music

Unit 4 (ASCAP)
see Warner-Chappell Music

United Artists Music Co., Inc.
6753 Hollywood Blvd.
Los Angeles, California 90028

## V

Valando Group (BMI)
1233 Avenue of the Americas
New York, New York 10036

Varon County (BMI)
see Tillis Tunes

Velle Int'l (ASCAP)
see MCA Music

Velvet Apple Music (BMI)
c/o Gelfand
1880 Century Park E., Ste. 900
Los Angeles, California 90067

VER Music (BMI)
    see Warner-Chappell Music

Virgin Music Ltd. (ASCAP)
    see Chappell & Co., Inc.

Virgin Songs (BMI)
    see EMI Music Publishing

Virgin Timber (BMI)
    see Polygram Music Publishing Inc.

Vitalturn (ASCAP)
    see Warner-Chappell Music

Vogue Music (BMI)
    see Welk Music Group

# W

Robert James Waller (ASCAP)
    Box 430
    Port Chester, New York 10573

Wallyworld Music (ASCAP)
    see Warner-Chappell Music

Warner-Chappell Music (ASCAP)
    10585 Santa Monica Blvd.
    Los Angeles, California 90025

Warner/Elektra/Asylum Music (BMI)
    see Warner-Chappell Music

Warner-Refuge Music Inc. (BMI)
    see Warner-Chappell Music

Warner-Tamerlane Music (BMI)
    see Warner-Chappell Music

Wasermusik
    see EMI Music Publishing

WB Music (ASCAP)
    see Warner-Chappell Music

Webo Girl (ASCAP)
    see Warner-Chappell Music

Donna Weiss Music (BMI)
    c/o Jerry B. Swartz
    4595 Wilshire Blvd., Ste. 10201
    Beverly Hills, California 90212

Welk Music Group
    1299 Ocean Avenue, Suite 800
    Santa Monica, California 90401

Wet Sprocket Songs (ASCAP)
    901 Third Street
    Suite 407
    Santa Monica, California 90403

Maurice White (ASCAP)
    4303 W. Verdugo Avenue
    Burbank, California 91505

White Oak Songs (ASCAP)
    156 5th Ave., Ste. 916
    New York, New York 10010

Who Is She Music (BMI)
    c/o Burton Goldstein
    100 Jericho Quadrangle
    Jericho, New York 11753

Wide Grooves (BMI)
    see Warner-Chappell Music

Wigged Music (BMI)
    c/o David Ross Craig
    213 Ave. of the Americas, Ste. 15
    New York, New York 10014

Wike (ASCAP)
    see Warner-Chappell Music

Wildcountry (ASCAP)
    see MCA Music

Willesden Music, Inc. (BMI)
    c/o Zomba House
    1348 Lexington Avenue
    New York, New York 10028

Williamson Music (ASCAP)
    see Warner-Chappell Music

Winding Brook Way Music (ASCAP)
    see Triple Star Music

Windswept Pacific (ASCAP)
    4450 Lakeside Dr., Ste. 200
    Burbank, California 91505

Wing It
    Address Unavailable

Wonderland Music (BMI)
    see Walt Disney Music

Word Life (ASCAP)
    see Chrysalis Music Group

Worksongs (ASCAP)
    see Almo/Irving

Write Treatage Music (ASCAP)
    207 1/2 First Avenue S.
    Seattle, Washington 98104

# Y
Yah-Mo (BMI)
    see Warner-Chappell Music

Yellow Elephant Music
    see Sony Music

You Can't Take It With You (ASCAP)
    9034 Sunset Blvd., Ste. 250
    Los Angeles, California 90069

Yreek (ASCAP)
    see Warner-Chappell Music

# Z
Zen of Iniquity (ASCAP)
    see Almo Music Corp.

Zomba House (ASCAP)
    137-139 W. 25th St, 8th Floor
    New York, New York 10001

Zomba Music (ASCAP)
    137-139 W. 25th St.
    New York, New York 10001

ISBN 0-8103-8498-1

90000